MEN
ON THE
CUSP

STEPPING UP, REACHING OUT, MOVING FORWARD

THOMAS NOLAN, LCSW

ARCHWAY
PUBLISHING

Archway Publishing books may be ordered through booksellers or by contacting:

Archway Publishing
1663 Liberty Drive
Bloomington, IN 47403
www.archwaypublishing.com
844-669-3957

ISBN: 978-1-6657-0100-6 (sc)
ISBN: 978-1-6657-0101-3 (hc)
ISBN: 978-1-6657-0102-0 (e)

Library of Congress Control Number: 2021911679

Print information available on the last page.

Archway Publishing rev. date: 6/9/2021

DEDICATION

To my wife, Arlene, whose love and inspiration has been at the center of my life and has taught me how to be a more unselfish partner.

To my children, Tommy, Jackie, Lyndea and Khrystle, who have given my life meaning and were my instructors in learning to be a better father.

Finally, to my mother Theresa and father Thomas, my two brothers John and Kevin, my sister Maribeth and the place where my learning began.

CONTENTS

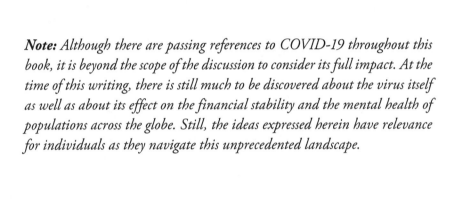

Note: *Although there are passing references to COVID-19 throughout this book, it is beyond the scope of the discussion to consider its full impact. At the time of this writing, there is still much to be discovered about the virus itself as well as about its effect on the financial stability and the mental health of populations across the globe. Still, the ideas expressed herein have relevance for individuals as they navigate this unprecedented landscape.*

INTRODUCTION:
CHANGE UNFOLDING

One day, I was meeting with a client, who was complaining about his wife and how women today want to control men's time, heaping demands on them that don't allow them any space to live. When I asked this client whether he thought it was true of all women, he responded that it applied to most women he knew. He continued to rant that his wife had a million projects around the house for him to do and that she wasn't even at the house as much as she should be. He said that if she didn't spend so much time on her business, he wouldn't have to watch the kids so much and he would have more time for himself. When I asked what he wanted to do that he couldn't do because of the situation, he wasn't sure. He just wanted more time to chill out.

What was it that brought on the complaint when he didn't even know how he would use the extra time anyway? And how had he generalized his objections about his wife to include most women?

Many men don't have control over their own lives and see the problem as being entirely outside of themselves. In these times of rapid change and evolving family structures many men are finding themselves afloat in a sea of confusion, not clear about their place or contribution anymore. For most of history, men have had much greater power than women. This is changing. Does this mean that men need to compromise their integrity or sense of value? Or, is it that they need to find — or redefine — what is a meaningful place now?

The world presents opportunities for us to make choices about how we want our lives to be. Today's society offers opportunities for all of us to have bigger lives and the possibility of many more choices.

How can a man begin to utilize these opportunities and take more control of his life? One answer is that he must challenge the old constructs of what being a man is to discover his greater potential. Of course, this is easier to preach than to do. Part of the journey involves understanding true power, not just in terms of things like physical force, but a fuller dimension of power — an internal force involving body, mind, and spirit. Power in this sense ensures that as external events present themselves we can truly depend on our internal strength and resources to create a more vibrant and meaningful way of being in the world, no matter what the world throws at us.

It's time to become intentional about designing a culture that benefits equally from clearer and more functional contributions from both men and women. We must wake up and assume our role as co-producers on this journey toward greater meaning and clarity. The gift of men and women being able to recognize each other's individual talents and strengths is in the ongoing discovery of complementary ways in which to co-contribute to the whole. As men, we need to work alongside women to create a safe world, rich with possibility for our children, for the future. It will involve an increased awareness of who we are, and the willingness to develop the vision of who we can become. It takes courage to leave our narrow, comfortable spheres that shield us even as they imprison us. Awakened to our true potential, and courageous in our willingness to open to it, we will become more effective in all of our roles, including as fathers.

STEPPING ONTO MY PATH

My first call to be a more engaged man came as a young adult, in the form of a depression. Having some difficulties in my relationships and feeling isolated, I was struggling. My way of handling it then was to try to put it out of my head. It would go away by ignoring it. That was my plan. But it got worse. I was critical of myself for feeling depressed and at other times blamed the people around me for causing it. Through a recommendation of a friend, I decided to seek professional help and it eventually paid off. With time, things began to make sense. There were parts of myself I had kept hidden and protected, and other areas I hadn't even discovered yet. I began to see a clearer direction for myself, and more important, I started feeling good about me. The whole experience deepened my awareness of who I was, and showed me the possibility of who I could become. I was presented with an opportunity to grow, and unknowingly took the first step. It started me on a journey that armed me with some tools that I would use for the rest of my life.

There are many reasons why a man decides to make changes in himself and his life. He becomes tired of his pain and suffering and wants to feel better. He may be forced to examine himself when an addiction becomes overwhelming or he runs into legal trouble. Or, one day, he may just realize that time is limited and he wants more from his life. Wanting to be a better father, a more loving partner, or a more effective leader may be the motivation.

Deep inside, most of us know that the answers don't lie outside of us. Our true power lies within. We start growing when we can connect to our inner power and become clearer about our direction. The men we admire are the men we want to be: He takes action when someone is being exploited. He musters the courage to admit his mistakes in a social or personal situation, choosing truth over fear. Or, maybe he risks being the target of a child's momentary wrath as he sets limits when they need protection, or when the child needs guidance in setting their own limits.

To understand why men must change in order to meet the change that is already upon us, it's important to understand something of the past and men's place in society — how we got here. Seeing men in the historical context of their usual role and the expectations that came with it will give us a dynamic picture of the interaction between a desire to expand personal boundaries and the container within which he was brought up, and continues to live and function.

IN GENERAL

Men's and women's roles were more specifically defined in the past and these roles worked pretty well prior to industrialization, at least for men. Women were confined to the home and to certain duties. Men were charged with fulfilling the role of breadwinner, and with that, they also had the power to make all the decisions. Today, of course this is no longer how things work. Tasks belong neither to one nor the other exclusively, and everyone feels freer to choose and create their own roles. Some men have embraced their freedom and are branching out into new arenas and responsibilities. The number of stay-at-home fathers has increased markedly and some men are taking their positions more seriously when it comes to supporting their families and spending more time with their children.

Not all men have been able to embrace and adjust to this changed world, even after decades.

In order to shift with the times, men must honestly ask themselves: What's stopping me from making choices that will create a fuller, happier life? What would have to change in order to make this happen?

Our cultural traditions have dictated the basic blueprint for gender roles and their structure has solidified as they have passed through the generations. Change can be very disruptive to people. Many of us are uncomfortable with possibility, even when it is positive, and prefer to stay with the status quo, even when is it not satisfying! We dig in. We resist change. In this book, we'll talk about that — and about paths to greater freedom, taking into account but not being confined by the past. One thing today's man will need to know is how to be in an honest, working relationship with his partner if he is part of a couple, and with the world. Many men don't know how to connect and share personal ideas and feelings.

I know from experience (personal and professional) that we can learn — whether young or late in life — what it means to nurture and be nurtured, to trust and be trusted, and to love and be loved. Yes, women have found greater freedom to expand their place in society, and men can feel left behind — or we can realize our potential too.

FATHERING

I am also speaking in this book to the importance of being more effective fathers. The men and women I mention in the book have begun to do the work to address being more inspiring supportive parents — individuals who walk the walk, or model what they teach, and know how to give direction when needed. I've had the opportunity to counsel many courageous men as they became happier, more relevant men and fathers. And I've worked with both women and men who yearn for the father presence in their own lives. I've learned a little something from all of them, as well as through my own passage into manhood. I've made mistakes and tried to benefit from them because as I have learned, there are no mistakes. Everything is an opportunity for us to grow.

I grew up in a world where men didn't question why they did what they did. They had less options about who they could become, and less tools and ways of thinking that could help them to become better fathers in a world beginning to change. As in most cultures, there was a small group of parents who could intuitively anticipate what boys needed and were aware, for example of the richness of emotion or the value of introspection in raising them. Most parents were unaware of a boy's potential and didn't have the tools that could effectively address those needs.

When I reached puberty, my repressed feelings were triggered by certain events and led to a rebelliousness that involved lighting fires in vacant lots, pulling neighborhood fire alarms and throwing rocks and breaking windows in homes. As I grew into adolescence, this angry behavior morphed into lying and stealing. I was too walled off from my feelings and would never admit that these were problems that I was willing to tackle. Fortunately, countering this were the positive forces of love and caring I encountered from people I met. These people helped me to value more the power of honesty and trust and feeling good about myself. Thankfully, my parent's values stuck in me and helped me in navigating through this period of my life.

As I got older I began to understand how these behaviors were critical pieces in learning who I was. Growing into adulthood, I continued to look from my life experience. As a man and a father, I spent too much time with my work and not enough time with my children. I have sometimes avoided making key decisions due to fear or people-pleasing. I am comfortable acknowledging my mistakes. It has been a journey.

Here in the book, you will meet divorced men, single men, married men, step-fathers, and men who have been separated from their children. In addition, you will meet some brave women who have had to shoulder all of the responsibility for the sake of the family. You will be introduced to children abandoned by their fathers and men who have turned their lives around after struggles with drugs or alcohol.

CHANGE IS STRESSFUL – SO IS STANDING STILL

Successful transition is rooted in the decision to deal with what's holding us back. As we know, stress is a normal part of life but if we don't manage it successfully, it can damage us physically, mentally, and emotionally. Being able to make real change in life usually involves an ability to manage stress. And what you cannot change, you can transform. We will talk about some strategies to reduce stress and manage areas of conflict more affectively.

What we cannot shift on our own, we can look to other men to teach us. We can talk with them or simply witness how they handle situations, and incorporate what we learn. Men who want to support their growth on a consistent basis may join with a men's group for regular support — or establish one. By creating a small community of like-minded people, growth can be multiplied in an environment that's safe and supportive. I've been part of a men's group for the past twenty years. It's been one of the most important experiences of my life. It has offered a forum to ask questions, open up about frustrations, and share personal joys and triumphs.

LOOKING AHEAD

It is my belief that a man's quest for a more complete life is fueled by his spirit or his soul. The soul is a dimension of a human being's principles and beliefs that drive actions and give them meaning. An evolving man is impassioned by his spirit, which calls forth his unique personal gifts toward bettering himself and all those around him in need of his care. What you believe can be so infectious that it can lift you and others into action toward love and the betterment of the planet.

Men and women have the opportunity to work together to improve the quality of life for themselves, and others. It starts small — in our own communities, and in our own families. It ultimately starts with ourselves. Men and women need to encourage each other to become more. Do we encourage our partners? This is an important element in a relationship that supports both partners and fosters a sense of working together.

In the following pages, you will learn strategies for change. You will also see that personal success is possible, and that success can be defined in a number of ways. You will gain a deeper understanding of the power of the human mind and heart in making change, and the importance of belief in realizing it. Stress is a part of life and I will share a number of techniques to reduce its effects — and to galvanize the energy hidden within it.

Looking ahead, you will find new ways of effective partnering, innovative ideas about contemporary parenting approaches, and fresh ideas for enriching your life. It is my hope you will walk away from the book with the very clear knowledge that we're not alone and that we can rely on each other for support in reaching our full potential.

— 1 —

THE OLD LESSONS DON'T APPLY ANYMORE

MAJOR SHIFTS

If you are fifty plus, you have some idea of the ways in which Western society has changed with the onslaught of technology and all that comes with globalization. If you are younger, you are living inside these shifts without a visceral understanding of what preceded it. For men to move forward and create more freedom in life, we must understand these societal changes historically, and appreciate our relationship to the past. These forces of change have had a significant impact on both sexes, sometimes causing us to question our roles and relationships in their wake. Both men and women are challenged to rise up to meet a changing world. Many men need to free themselves from their emotional prisons, allowing their feelings to enrich their experience of life, both at home and in business. Women and men want to continue envisioning broader, more expanded possibilities for jobs, in relationships, and in dealing with life's stresses. Together, they want to orient toward joy. We begin with a historical overview.

WHERE WE WERE

Throughout most of history, family structure and development were pretty fixed and clear. Things tend to run smoothly when they're defined.

Most successful sports teams succeed because everyone has defined roles and contributes uniquely to the team's performance. In a good drama, the various actors play their parts to make sense of the whole story. Any working machine consists of individual components that work together to perform the specific function. Likewise, families function more efficiently when their roles are defined. Prior to industrialization, everyone knew their place and also what was expected. Roles were defined by the outside in. For example, the father was seen as the breadwinner and the authority figure in the household, while the mother served as the nurturer. The father usually worked outside the home but locally, and the mother stayed in the home, cared for the children, and ran the daily operations of the home. It was a smaller, more contained experience of life with limited contact with the broader, more complex world. Family values and beliefs were usually religiously based and stemmed from the churches, synagogues, and mosques. Beliefs were clear and everyone knew their place. Of course, "their place" likely was a prison for some — both men and women. So when things began to change, there was excitement alongside the fear.

The paradigm-shifting period of the 1960s and 1970s had its roots in industrialization and did not appear out of the blue. This era brought about a radical questioning of cultural values. This process of dramatic inquiry resulted in a great upheaval in a society that began challenging its own belief systems and behaviors. Values were reassessed, and the map was no longer clear for gender roles and parenting perspectives, at least not in terms of being in accord with a single, coherent value system. Some called it the "me" generation, because of the focus on the individual. It not only involved the youth questioning traditional values, but adults wanting more freedom for themselves as well. Both men and women experimented with breaking out of traditional gender roles.

The inequality that had been long accepted between the sexes in the workplace, education, and sexuality was finally being challenged. Women, having had a taste of the workplace when so many men were called to fight in World War II, began moving out of the home and pursuing professions that had traditionally been the realm of men. And as women's roles were beginning to evolve, men also had greater freedom though they weren't as moved to challenge their traditional roles. The perception and the reality of their gender roles remained the same despite the changing landscape. Women were moving toward freedom — out of servitude — but it wasn't as clear what men were moving toward. The sense was, in part, that they were giving up something. It was better to hold on to what they had. On many levels, this sense still guides many men, even if they hide it well.

Alongside the shifts in gender roles, communication and technology were beginning to explode. People began to have contact with the larger human culture on a more regular basis. Traveling out of one's local community became more commonplace, less expensive, more convenient. People had greater access to a broad spectrum of ways of being and they were increasingly being stimulated by new or different ideas.

A greater freedom of thought was being embraced by individuals and as a result by institutions by which people were educated, governed, and guided. Many beliefs and traditions previously held sacred began to be questioned. The foundation of the nuclear family became part of this process of inquiry. Both children and adults were trying on new roles. At the same time, social tensions also were rising. The struggle for racial equality and the struggle for gender equality were parallel processes. And, as the status quo started to become dismantled, many people were confused, angry, and anxious. All transition inspires these responses — even change for the good.

As usual, men were benefitting much more economically from the changes than women. Even though since 1935 women had increased their participation in college education from 40 percent to 70 percent, they experienced no practical results from these gains yet. With the increase in divorce rates, women paid the price economically because they were often strapped with the burden of single parenthood.

So, despite the radical changes in society, men's roles basically remained the same, though women began to gain a foothold in education and in the workplace. Again, this parallels the experience of people of color in many ways. Women benefitted from social and political support from groups such as the National Organization of Women (NOW), which consistently championed the rights of women.

Still, men continued to hold the institutional and political power, and as long as they had this, they felt little need to change. The status quo is difficult to give up, especially when it affords you greater access to money, power, and influence.

THE TURN OF THE CENTURY

Through the 1980s and 1990s women continued to make gains in all areas of life. As women gained a foothold in the jobs market, men began to feel the competition. One thing was becoming clear; women were in the public sphere to stay.

In the late 1990s through the early 2000s, things became more difficult for the entire working population. A series of recessions hit the economy, making jobs less available. Companies were downsizing, especially in the construction and manufacturing sectors. Some men were faced with fighting for shrinking opportunities within a structure that was gradually inching them out, or seeking to redefine themselves. Choosing the latter option would involve creating new paradigms, which is the harder choice, at least ostensibly. Most men were unable to respond to a society that was demanding a new way to look at its needs culturally and economically. How do men become more relevant in a society craving new structure, creative political and social solutions, and healing action?

HERE WE ARE

The understanding of gender today wouldn't be complete without a clear picture of how open and diversified views of gender have become.

With less rigidity in defining roles and more sharing of traditional characteristic traits, gender roles are seen by most people as the same with little or no formal distinction between the sexes. We can choose who we want to be. Many understand gender to be fluid. Imagine that conversation happening on Father Knows Best!

Even those who see themselves as traditional have shifted in subtle ways. An article in the National Geographic entitled "Rethinking Gender" states: "A recent survey of a thousand millennials ages 18 to 34 found that half of them think gender is a spectrum, and some people fall outside conventional categories." (The Gender Revolution, Jan. 2017)

The development of more sophisticated technologies in genetics and brain science have led to a better understanding of how we come to be male and female from a biological standpoint, which we will discuss in the next chapter. For now, the question is: Are there inherent biological/ psychological/sociological parameters for men and women, and should they affect how men and women "choose" their paths?

GENDER AND THE ECONOMY: HIS-STORY

THE ECONOMY

It's one thing to lose a job for a couple of months, and another to be without one for an extended period of time. For some men, it may affect making an alimony or child support payment, or paying down a student loan. For others, the loss of work involves other financial pressures, such as rent, mortgage payments, or general household expenses. In an atmosphere of limited jobs and the competition with women for those very same positions, how do they move to get back on their feet and feel more confident in an environment where old structures traditionally supporting men are harder to negotiate? This question is, of course, being amplified across the world as we all try to reimagine our lives even as COVID redefines our mobility.

MEET JIM:

Jim, thirty-five, is a single father with full custody of his fourteen-year-old son. He had been contemplating leaving his job due to boredom and ongoing conflict with one particular co-worker. One day, his position was eliminated. Over the next six months, he went on numerous interviews struggling to find work, but to no avail. It began to affect all of his financial responsibilities, including mortgage payments and utility bills. Eventually, his unemployment ran out.

He was referred to me by his mother with whom I had worked previously. She said he was very stubborn and would tell her he didn't need help. Still, he agreed to meet. At the first session, I just listened and asked some questions, alert to opportunities to make it safe for him to be more open.

In subsequent sessions, it became clear that Jim felt lots of frustration. This frustration was causing a lot of anxiety and inhibiting any efforts to get into positive action. To lower his anxiety, we did some relaxation exercises and used some breathing techniques. Continuing to encourage him to use these exercises, we spent the next couple of meetings focusing on his strengths, which included his loyalty, intelligence, and willingness to work hard.

Being more motivated, and after acknowledging the limited opportunities to find work within his field, was he willing to explore other options? We found he had lots of practical skills around fixing machinery and making home repairs. He began to solicit these types of jobs. Eventually, he found a part-time, mobile mechanic's position doing oil changes, and he took on some odd jobs servicing computers (a personal hobby) for a few friends. His confidence began to grow. He wanted more.

With a more positive framework in place, he agreed to see a business coach and ask for help. He also targeted a local mechanic to apply for work. We spoke about the importance of expanding his field of possible choices for work, that he had a number of capabilities and interests. Since he wasn't sure of what he wanted to do, he thought that meeting with the coach would be a good first step. After a few days, he landed a job in a new field. He became more hopeful, even saying: "If this position doesn't work out, I know what I can do now to eventually find a job that fits my passion." Jim's willingness to explore outside the box of what had once defined him, and to seek help, gave him the impetus to find meaningful work.

What Jim Learned: He learned to calm his anxiety through some simple breathing and relaxation exercises. He expanded his job possibilities by taking an inventory of his personal/professional attributes as well as going outside his normal scope of search and hiring a business coach. He also began to develop a new resiliency, being able to bounce back from disappointment. He envisioned options beyond the same-old territory and embraced his own confidence and authenticity as important attributes.

When our identity is so strongly attached to our work, as is most men's, a change in our job status can have a powerful effect. The stress and the feelings of loss begin to chip away at self-esteem. You were working... producing and making a living. The next thing you know, you're jobless, having difficulty finding work in your field, and living off whatever savings you may have, or charging your life on credit cards. This affects your feelings about yourself, especially your sense of worth. Men have been taught through the generations that their value is in their work as providers. Feeling unmoored, many men get discouraged and don't know where to turn for help. They may hold feelings inside and become depressed. They've been taught from early on to be independent and self-sufficient. Asking for help, they think, shows weakness, dependency, and vulnerability. They have learned that these are qualities that should remain hidden — even from ourselves.

When crises occur in the work environment, it can be seen as a time for informed action, and more positive reframe. Again, this is the new normal — and everyone is suffering the effects of a slow-dripping global trauma. Resiliency and an inner sense of empowerment are more important than ever. Reaching out for support is also important.

This is the perfect time to mine fresh new possibilities. To begin, it is helpful to find a place where one can open oneself and be encouraged to verbalize feelings, rather than holding them inside. It can be the beginning of where a man can start to release his need to be self-sufficient and learn that vulnerability isn't a weakness. This is the moment for men to embrace their dimensionality, not only taking into account facts and data, but giving serious consideration to personal aspirations, fears, and passions.

Here's a question to ask yourself: What do you consider to be two good personal qualities about yourself and what two qualities would you like to get better at? You can use the opportunity to dip below the surface. Men who find themselves struggling with a loss of identity because of job loss can seek counseling, a safe place where feelings are validated and fears faced.

Besides making contact with professionals and support groups, you can reach out and identify friends who are doing okay in their own careers, and find out what they are doing differently. You want to find resources with new solutions, and not recycled approaches. We are in unprecedented times; old ideas don't likely apply. I believe and have witness the ways men can overcome their self-limiting beliefs and find meaningful ways to connect to the world and feel productive. Many men are beginning to see the value of seeking help, of opening up, and of getting in touch with their potential competencies.

MEET SAL:

Sal, who is forty-eight years old and is married with a fourteen-year-old son, has been in the telecommunications field for his whole career. Being under the threat of downsizing from his company for several years, he was finally released. He took the loss really hard. Feeling demoralized and discouraged about the prospects for another job, he eventually agreed to meet with me. Despite his reluctance to get help (he kept saying that he didn't need it), he began to soften when he realized that his stubbornness and fear of asking for help were okay. The realization and acceptance of his false sense of independence freed him to move through it, and into a place that could be of more benefit to him. He began to notice how he protected himself even from being more successful in his present career, and how his confidence was being undermined by his protected stance.

As well as continuing our work together, I suggested he meet with a local church group that had regular meetings dedicated to readying adults to apply for jobs. I suggested that they might be able to work with him in a more concrete way with his job search. His feelings of frustration and fear had eaten away at his confidence, and it felt good to him to be able to express himself freely with other men. Later, this group helped him prepare a resume that better reflected his newfound confidence, and he learned some unique ways to prepare for interviews. He landed two jobs within the next two months, and was feeling good about himself. He was very grateful that he had pursued the help he needed.

What Sal Learned: He gained insight into how he had limited his potential for more productive and satisfying work by avoiding a very important component of his experience — his feelings. He began to move through not only his present blockage, but understood how his fears had been affecting other areas of his life. Reaching out to a local church group was positive as a practical resource in targeting specific change. Reaching out in general unlocked a new realm of internal strength and connection.

MEET MATTHEW:

Matthew is sixty-two years old and a single father of two adult children. He worked his whole career in his own business as an insurance salesperson and financial advisor. Although it paid the bills and put both children through school, he had been unhappy in his job for many years. It felt empty and he was just going through the motions. He knew he was capable of so much more. He had first come to see me some years earlier, working on a problem with a severe addiction to prescription meds. With the help of our work and regular attendance at AA meetings, he was sober.

Now, he came into therapy wanting to focus on his unhappiness and boredom at work. With lots of experience in addiction recovery, he wanted to do counseling. He had gained experience working in a mental health clinic with people in recovery, and was ready for more.

The problem was that he was hesitant to leave a job that made him a good living and provided safety for him. Could he take the leap? Could he do what he really wanted or would he stay safe? Once a man finds his purpose, he wants more for himself. Usually this can begin with him connecting to his passion and using this as his guide to move forward. We all know men who like what they do. They feel good about themselves as men, and always look to do their jobs well. Matthew wanted to be able to tell that story.

Matthew and I met a few times for the purpose of getting him moving. I asked him what his fear was about. He said it was uncertainty. He wanted everything mapped out. Later in our conversations, he admitted to being afraid of making mistakes. He wanted to make the "perfect choice." He worried about what people would say and think. I asked him what he would tell his son if his son came to him for advice about taking an IT position that he wanted, but wasn't sure that he could do. Matthew immediately responded: "I'd tell him to go for it! You'll learn as you go!" Matthew left the session energized, and two days later he met a life coach. He signed up the next day!

Sometimes, one gets to a tipping point and decides to take that leap. All of a sudden, once the decision is made, the universe seems to present solutions. Or, one begins to notice situations that were always there but out of awareness. Matthew had held himself so bound to his fears that he couldn't see a possible solution.

What Matthew Learned: He admitted to his fear so he could move beyond it. He took the advice he imagined giving to his son! Having the awareness that someone else could do it, gave him the confidence to take a risk. He reoriented to desire more than safety and signed up for a course that would support him in that choice.

We also worked to expand his feeling experience as a traditional male by asking him to explore the feelings under the feelings. (We'll discuss this process more fully later on.)

———————————————

Successful adults contribute to society through meaningful and productive work. It's part of what defines them as people. Men and women's roles have been narrowly defined for most of history. Women didn't suddenly decide to change. A confluence of historical factors primed the opportunity. The Industrial Revolution made traditional tasks in the home less time-consuming and, in addition, jobs outside the home opened up during the WWII, and many women got a taste of accomplishment and finding meaning in work outside the home. This and the growing role of technology have created new opportunities. But men also can take advantage of the increased openness of the culture.

MEET PATRICK:

Patrick's marriage had ended because of his drinking. Like many alcoholics, he blamed his wife for his problems. He was angry and confused. He had tried AA twice but without success. He couldn't get past the first step — that he was powerless over alcohol. But, recently he had become more desperate and he came to realize that he couldn't do it by himself. Having some difficulty understanding this idea of a power greater than ourselves, he did the only thing he knew, he started going back to church to explore his confusion.

One Sunday morning he heard a sermon about it being our responsibility to care for those less fortunate than ourselves. He thought of his child and her needs. Up to this point, he had resented paying alimony and child support because of his anger toward his ex-wife. Listening to the sermon, he had the realization that he didn't want his child to suffer, and that he was selfishly focusing on himself and his own needs. After reviewing his own economic situation, he wanted to become more accountable as a father even though his own budget would be tighter. He decided to be more responsible about his alimony and child support payments. He wanted to do the right thing. He was given the opportunity to be different, and he made a choice. It felt good.

What Patrick Learned: He understood the personal value of being more financially responsible for his child. He expanded his sense of "fathering." He allowed himself to feel empathy toward his daughter, something that had been obscured by his anger and frustration toward her mother, and then blocked by his own guilt and avoidance.

Anger and frustration are obstacles for many men. We were not taught to access the whole spectrum of emotions. In fact, many of us were taught that feelings were wrong or weak, the purview of women. Our lessons included:

When hurt, show no vulnerability — be angry or emotionally distant. When confused or fearful, show no weakness. When faced with the feelings of others, be logical and try to fix their problems rather than empathize with them. When faced with feelings of intimacy, protect yourself.

THE GROWTH OF TECHNOLOGY

Technology is part of the social framework one must grapple with in order to change. Its effects have been felt in every aspect of our lives from how we eat and socialize, to how we do business and communicate.

The rise of technology and the massive amounts of information that need to be processed on a daily basis have had a huge influence on values and communication over the past forty years. Some people have been quick to adapt, while others have had a hard time adjusting. The quantity and speed of data being exchanged and the ease with which people can connect anywhere at any time is awesome — and for some of us overwhelming.

Of course, not everyone has been able to keep up. What is second nature for some is still challenging to others. There are those who refuse to use technology either because they're frustrated by it, or they believe it's too impersonal. If the normal generation gap created misunderstandings among family members a couple of generations ago, technological shifts have tripled and quadrupled the gaps. It isn't just ideas that are different now, but how those ideas are communicated.

Still, the benefits are many. Technology has increased production of goods and services across the board, contributed to the advancement of creative ideas, and added to the comfort and fluidity with which a society functions. It has opened up new worlds of information and communication. On the other hand, some would argue that technology, with its vast wealth of information and data-focused nature, has caused a kind of dehumanization from a social and psychological perspective. We are both remarkably connected and disconnected. We were distancing long before it became mandated.

People are more connected to their devices and spend less time involved in human interaction. This reliance on our phones has created complications in many areas of our lives. A recent report on 60 Minutes featured Google product manager, Tristan Harris, who explained: "Silicon Valley programmers are engineering your phone and its apps for you to check in more and more." That companies can monitor how many times you check in to your phone and what your preferences are reinforces our dependence. Advertisers are profiting from this, of course, as are the technology companies themselves, keeping us hooked. Our brains respond immediately and repeatedly to the pings and beeps and flashes. And now, of course, we are truly dependent as we accommodate the threat that COVID poses. Still, there are things we can do to mitigate the takeover of our brain!

The speed at which things are changing — have already changed — has overwhelmed some, and contributed to difficulty in processing new ideas. Trying to manage the massive content bombarding us can cause stress and depression, and can also translate into physical symptoms, sometimes leading to serious illness. Our brain needs to constantly adapt to keep pace. Never has it been so apparent that we need to really discern what we can change and what we can't — and begin to figure out how to take responsibility for all of the areas we *can*.

1. The most basic realization is in acknowledging the dehumanizing aspects as well as the advantages of technology and the consequences. The compulsion in our society to get immediate results puts added pressure on the individual to organize and understand experiences immediately. Such impossible emotional timelines tend to increase stress, which can affect the accuracy of what we perceive. If we can't "experience" in the present because

things are happening too fast, we don't completely absorb the data and so lose the quality of our experiences. We need to become mindful of this process, of what is happening around us and within us, and begin to take charge of our time and decisions. Take an inventory of your life. Are you productive and happy? What would help you to better use and benefit from technology — rather than being used by it?

2. Slow down. Find ways to lighten your daily activities. For example, one client decided to cut her morning workouts from four to two mornings a week, and use the time to sleep later on the "off" mornings. And, although another client could have used the extra money, he cut his overtime by three hours a week to return home early and just unwind. And, still another took a break from her online work to read and relax for an hour a day three days a week. One client decided after we had done some work on it that the kitchen didn't have to be perfectly straightened up every night. This reduced her stress and eventually became more important to her than being such a fastidious housekeeper. Small changes can make significant differences in the quality of life.

It is essential to carve out ways to build in mindful pauses in our day-to-day life in order to improve the time we have.

We will discuss other techniques and strategies for dealing with making clearer choices and reducing stress and conflict in Chapter 5. Reducing stress is central to change.

If it's increasingly difficult to comprehend your world, it is difficult to find your place in it. To make good choices about how our individual roles might evolve, we have to understand the social and technological dynamics at work behind the scenes. Those challenged to become part of the growing technology can benefit from some support in the community. Many are ready and willing to learn if approached with patience by those willing to teach.

Before the growth of technology, life took place in more limited geographical areas. People lived their lives and worked locally. Of course, we hardly remember that time. In this moment, there are more opportunities for evolution than ever before, more exposure to a wider spectrum of people and cultures, and therefore exposure to a greater diversity of perspectives. When life was lived more locally, the opportunities for imagining our potential beyond the scope of the small town, the village, the limited number of people with whom we had contact, were few. Life was simpler, for better and worse.

Expansion has downsides. Life can be more hectic and complicated. In a 2014 article in the AARP Bulletin told the story of one man's 2012 cardiac event. His youngest child was going to start in a local college in Phoenix, but he himself had to take a job in Seattle. He explained, "My stress levels were off the charts!" He spent five days in the ICU and had two titanium stents put in. This incident caused him to completely reevaluate his life. I'm sure there were other factors contributing to Jay's heart condition, but the stress of travel and the distance from his family were new stressors that many men experience at this time in history. Trying to keep up with everything challenges health and decreases the amount of contact time for many families and thus the support for each member.

Also, because of the hectic nature of our lives many men and women invest more time at their jobs completing their responsibilities and tying up loose ends. Because of powerful economic and job pressures, many people don't get to stop to take those mindful pauses.

Change is constant, though it ebbs and flows with varying intensity. With any kind of change, there comes a period of adaptation and disorientation. We are — all 7 billion of us — in the midst of that now. Stress is generated when people decide or have to leave old structures that are comfortable and familiar, even when the new ones are more functional. Historically, men have been in the power seat. Why give that up? Perhaps for a position in society that is less powerful? Won't this mean giving up many of the privileges that have been previously enjoyed? Won't this mean a loss of identity? These questions are being asked across race and economic status too. The truth is, when everything is changing around you, you either decide to grow or you become obsolete. You can stay entrenched or seize the opportunity to adapt.

Society has evolved and will continue to do so. The societal shifts have encouraged both men and women to adjust to changing needs, to give the best of themselves and their unique talents. Some of the traditional ways of being a man don't work anymore. We must learn from the past, and recapture what strengths were there, and apply these strengths in our present culture. We need to also acquire new beliefs and behaviors that will enable us to use our gifts and talents.

We can't live in the past. The beliefs about roles and the individual's place in society don't make sense anymore. As our ideas of freedom and equality continue to grow and develop, and technology exerts its influence on the expansion of ideas, many of the old ways will continue to become obsolete and limiting for men. They won't be relevant. We need to take with us the important values from the past as we envision the stepping stones that will raise us to our greater potential as men and women.

— 2 —

MEN AND WOMEN

F orty or fifty years ago, the idea of dedicating a chapter to the differences between a man and a woman would have seemed absurd. It wouldn't have even been a question. A man worked to support his family and was the authority figure in the home. As in the old shows — think, *Father Knows Best* and *My Three Sons* — the father refereed many family clashes, while periodically offering timely pearls of wisdom. The woman was the homemaker, the nurturer, and the heart of the family. She could not exert overt power; he could not show vulnerability. Roles and identities were clear and rigid.

Today, many factors have blurred that clear distinction. As we have discussed, the rise of the women's rights movement and the questioning of the traditional roles of men and women reflect the shift. Along with these factors, science has expanded the understanding of biological and social boundaries regarding sex and gender. New discoveries in the field of genetics give us a better understanding of the physical basis of how the sex of a person is formed, and what genes control it. For instance, rather than sexual identity being a random act, gender can be chosen. So much so, that genetic engineering can be used to select the sex of a child by direct manipulation of the embryo. Many questions arise as to whether these methods are ethical or "good" for society or for us. On the positive side, such freedom of choice could serve to avoid the transmission of genetic disorders, though this is also controversial. Such freedom is a challenge once we begin to imagine that we have the knowledge or right to judge as a worthwhile life. Would Stephen Hawking have been spared given the choice? And, who is to judge what is a life worth living anyway? Only those who are living it, perhaps.

Science has opened up major questions in the area of sexuality. The number of people choosing to change their sexual orientation from the one assigned at birth is increasing. According to a 2016 survey conducted by The Williams Institute (UCLA School of Law), the transgender population has doubled from 0.3 percent to 0.6 percent in just over a decade. This represents 1.4 million people in the United States. What appears on the outside to be male or female is sometimes experienced differently from within. Many of the differences that once constituted a so-called complementary quality for the sexes have shifted alongside burgeoning knowledge about identity. This is a complicated and exciting sphere of investigation, but it is outside the scope of the present discussion. I bring it up only to say that paradigms are shifting across all dimensions. What we are focusing on here is how traditional roles for men and women have served as standard directions on the social compass for generation upon generation; something that no longer holds true.

While women have been expanding their choices, and finding a true balance for themselves (after eons of repression and suppression), men in general, have been less clear and less motivated to grow in their roles and expand their own personal experience of themselves. In part, this stems from the fact that men have dominated women throughout history and have felt less of a need to change. It is a frightening prospect for many men, even as everything has already shifted around us. We see this everywhere, the digging in of our heals in the attempt to hold onto the old (no matter our age). Exceptions do exist, though. We have seen a rise in the number of house-husbands and caretakers, for example. The American Psychological Association reports that there was a 50 percent increase in the number of stay-at-home dads between 2003 and 2006. Some men remained at home because their wives had a better paying job but the majority reported wanting to remain at home because they wanted to bond with their child and they actually felt more in tune with the role.

So different from decades ago, and already forgotten by most, men have learned and continue to learn to share household responsibilities. Because of a tight economy and the fast pace of life, and women no longer being willing to be relegated to roles not of their own choosing, responsibilities mount, and families can't meet their overall needs unless both parents share household chores. And, most women will no longer stand for having sole responsibility for keeping up the home. My client, Ray, for example, considers himself a traditional male, but has been slowly making changes in his own relationship. Taking early retirement, he enjoys playing golf and working outside in the yard. His wife remains in a job she loves as a counselor and budding entrepreneur. Since she is still working, and also caring for a sick relative, he has assumed the shopping duties and is in charge of keeping order in the house.

PHYSIOLOGICAL DIFFERENCES

A number of comparative studies of males and females from conception through early childhood have shown some major differences in brain development. For example, beginning at birth females hear better than males, especially at the higher frequencies (1000-4000 mz), which is connected to the speech centers (Sax, 2017). Maybe this is part of the reason why girls tend to speak earlier than boys. In boys, the language centers in the left hemisphere (logical side) develop first, whereas in girls, the language centers in both hemispheres (logical and creative) progress simultaneously.

Boys and girls initially mature differently in their vision. Two types of cells, M and P (M is larger), connect differently to the rods and cones of the eye. In newborn boys, the M cells connect in greater amounts to the rods, which tune into the movement of objects. In baby girls, the P-cells connect to the cones that focus on the detail of the objects. In *Boys Adrift*

(2017), Sax reports, "A richly textured doll will be more appealing than a moving truck if your system favors P-cells, as is the case in females." The book describes that in studies where mobiles are in motion over the cribs of newborns, boys tend to focus in on the movement, rather than on the face of the person standing next to the mobile, as girls would.

Differences between boys and girls continue to extend into the childhood years. In children from seven to seventeen, feelings mature differently. According to Sax (2017): "In boys, as in men, the part of the brain where emotions happen (the amygdala) is not well connected to the part of the brain where verbal processing and speech happens — unlike the situation with girls and women." It's no wonder that difficulty in expressing emotions is more prevalent in men. The connection to the amygdala exists at a more primitive level in boys, and the expression is a more visceral and spontaneous one.

See what fits! Here is a table I've assembled that maps some general strengths for each gender:

Women:	Men:
See big picture and focus on situational thinking	Spatial thinking (pattern recognition)/
Good Listener	Problem-solving
Multi-tasking	Single-task focus
Social thinking and interactions	Abstract thinking and task-orientation
More empathic and comprehensive	Larger parietal lobe-better in math
Emphasis on left amygdala-internal functions	Rt. Amygdala- external functions

More attuned to words and sounds; learning languages	Better coordination and control; Faster reaction times
Better recall of names, faces pictures	Better sense of direction; visual and spatial
Higher coordination of multiple senses	Higher visual sensing; turned on by what they "see"
	Brain wired for greater risk-taking

In relationship:

Importance of being emotionally and physically connected	Sex is more physically based and slower to be integrated emotionally

These recent findings begin to support some of the long-standing views of men and women as unique and complementary. As you can see, tendencies such as multi-tasking versus single focus or internal functioning versus external functioning balance one another, whereas better recall or better sense of direction are comparative, and can also be seen as individual strengths. Relationship differences also reflect different biological predispositions, such as more development in the higher regions of the brain (cortex) in girls and higher connection to the amygdala in boys.

Again, from a physiological perspective, certain developmental processes happen differently. The example of the amygdala not being very well connected to the verbal centers in boys can partially explain why many boys are slower to develop certain emotional states than girls. Again, boys linger in a more primitive, externally focused emotional state.

Some of these differences point to the importance of learning to approach boys and girls differently. For girls, hearing sensitivities especially in the higher frequencies may lead to a perception they're being yelled at, for example. To account for this, we can speak more softly to girls in order to be understood correctly. Likewise, to expect a boy to connect readily with his emotions when his brain is focused more on movement and action might not always work. We might decide to describe his experience through the language of movement using his view of the world to teach emotion. In this view, boys and girls are valued equally, but how they learn best can be accounted for by appreciating their developmental differences.

PERSPECTIVES ON MEN AND WOMEN USING OTHER LENSES

We find similar conceptions to the recent findings in brain science in numerous belief systems. For centuries, Eastern thought has held that the complementary male and female natures exist within each person in the form of yin (female energy) and yang (male energy). Everything that we see around us, including all matter, is made of energy called "Qi" (chee). "Qi" takes two forms, yin and yang. Master Chunyi Lin explains, "These two energies exist together in every person. A good balance of them isn't necessarily an equal balance, but is unique to each individual. Yin represents something feminine, passive (receptive), and spiritual; Yang represents something masculine, active and physical. Examples of Yin would be woman, water, spiritual life and earth. Examples of Yang would be man, fire, the physical body and sky" (Spring Forest Qigong, Level 1, 2000).

PSYCHOLOGY

Carl Jung posited a similar concept by noting the animus (male) and anima (female) energies within each of us. Both exist in what Jung refers to as the collective unconscious. This is a construct that contains all the unconscious male and female impulses, memories, and emotions (archetypes) common to all species and that originates in the inherited structure of the brain. The collective unconscious both transcends and is a part of the individual's personal psyche.

The animus is the unconscious male energy in women and the anima is the unconscious female energy in men. The development of a man's anima happens over a lifetime if he's open. It moves him into his inner being where he learns increased sensitivity and intuitiveness. This movement tends to balance out and soften his animus, which is identified with the physical and the external. Both the anima and the animus have positive and negative sides to their construct and both are key to the development of the "self." Here again the perspective highlights the uniqueness of, and distinction between, feminine and masculine energies.

The notion of male/female complementarity within each of us takes the unisexual construct of a man or woman and enhances its focus. Rather than designating these constructs as male or female, we can see them as a series of paired opposites that make up the whole. For example, directive/receptive could be a pair representing a complementary description of behaviors that exist within the same person. The balance of each quality would be different depending on the individual. This view expands the potentialities of both men and women. It rebalances the concept of gender neutrality to one that views difference and uniqueness as a positive supposition. Differences don't limit us, they enrich us and make us viably essential to our complementary half. The view that a man's "anima" is valuable and essential for his complete development challenges the view that a man is only a male when he embodies the qualities of the traditionally defined male energy. And, obviously, women can have a strong, assertive side that enhances their nature. The idea of encompassing both gender identities rather than splitting them represents a powerful shift in our thinking. A freedom to explore and unify these possibilities becomes the driving force, rather than limiting our views and defining the roles of men and women in narrow ways. This lens offers a new frame. Rather than "us against them," it is inclusive — them within us — for both men and women.

The freedom to choose from an array of personal qualities gives us the possibility to embrace particular complementary traits as we desire. The balance may differ in line with biological and gender uniqueness, but it doesn't mean that men and women need to be confined to living within those lines. A man, for example, can choose to stay home with his kids even when it doesn't come easily at first. After all, he wasn't "taught" about this possibility, and perhaps his brain works against him. Still, his situation or his inner disposition may determine this as a better choice for him. He may learn to appreciate the difficulties of raising children but also the great rewards of this level of bonding. A woman may not want to work as well as care for the day-to-day activities of the children, but it may be necessary. She will succeed in finding a satisfactory balance the more she practices. People can be more of what they want to be.

The challenge for men is being open to developing their softer, more sensitive side, and believing in the possibility that it can expand what we can become as men, and what we can give to our children as fathers. As men, this is a real challenge because we have been rooted in a powerful, safe position for centuries that neither invited nor necessitated change. The time has come.

MEET MARCEL:

Marcel, who is sixty-two years old, learned to develop his sensitivity through various challenges in his life. He came to the United States from Cuba in 1966. It was early in Fidel Castro's rule, and Marcel's father had spent time in jail as a political prisoner.

I asked him what he thought it meant to become a man, and when he thought he had become one. He said it was different for everyone, but that his transformation occurred when he came to this country from Cuba.

He had to leave his friends, extended family, and everything he knew to move with his family. He spoke no English. Just thirteen years old, and the oldest of three, he took care of his younger brother and sister, while his parents worked at any jobs they could in order to feed the family. He spoke with certainty, "That's when I grew up! I made sure they ate, and got back and forth to school. It was hard for me, but I felt we were all in this together as a family."

Marcel was a traditional man in the grip of the "macho" role, with a limited ability to express his emotions. Initially, he was teased in school because of his English and he retreated more into himself. He withdrew even further when he developed severe acne at about fifteen years old. He remembered, "Just when I started speaking better English and feeling a little more comfortable, I was tortured by some of the other kids about the acne! I felt bad about myself, but who could I talk to?" At the time, his parents couldn't afford to take him to a dermatologist.

Moving into adulthood his parents worked hard to put him through technical school, and he found a job he enjoyed and was good at. Later on, he got married and had a child. He explained, "I didn't change diapers. That wasn't a man's role." He did do some chores around the house, he quickly added, "I grew up that way."

Marcel and his family eventually moved to a new town, where he found lots of happiness, but he still had no close friends. And he continued to have this sense of feeling constricted. One day, his wife mentioned that a friend's husband had attended a men's weekend through one of the local churches. Not a particularly religious person, Marcel wasn't initially attracted to the opportunity, but the man resonated with his experience and so paid Marcel a visit. Marcel was hesitant, suspicious, and nervous.

Change doesn't happen by itself. Unless we have something to motivate us, to drive us to push through the boundaries of our comfort zones, we will not likely make the move. But something inside Marcel urged him to take the risk.

He felt uneasy entering the church basement, but as he listened to the first presenter speak openly about the difficulties in his own life, his nervousness began to subside. He could relate to this guy. He was happy to report, "Someone else felt the way that I did!" The longer he stayed, the more he realized that men had feelings and could express them. He saw that the men treated one another with kindness and sensitivity in the group, that they could compete with each other on the basketball court during lunch break, and then listen and share their innermost feelings during the talks and discussion groups. He felt parts of himself coming to life! An emotional release began to occur. He was scared, but at the same time there was a sense of comfort that felt new and inviting. Gradually, Marcel started sharing his own feelings and experiences, letting them out. He saw too that his expressions touched other men and encouraged them to connect within themselves and with each other.

Soon, he was sharing on a regular basis with different groups of men and exposing them to what he found so helpful for himself. He wanted to give back, so other men could be connected to the deeper potential in themselves. Allowing himself to participate in the group meeting, and a new experience, he discovered a deeper, fuller sense of what it meant to be a man for himself. To be a man means to be passionate about living an involved life and finding your unique purpose.

What Marcel Learned: He moved out from under the protective shield he had developed as an immigrant and opened himself to more connected experience. He was able to find that deeper connection as a man and develop his fuller potential as a human being. While remaining a traditional man, he learned that life can present other opportunities to evolve a broader view. He found that he had the courage to become more open and see that his experience also touched others.

RITES OF MANHOOD

Most societies have structures that initiate their young into adulthood. Such initiation in some cases represents centuries of experience and belief about what it means to be a man, and what each individual culture expects and needs from its people. Expectations may range from the demanding and arduous practices of ancient cultures to more benign practices of today.

MEET SHADRACK:

In a small village in Kenya, Shadrack, a fourteen-year-old from the Bukusu tribe, prepares for the ancient ritual initiating him to adulthood. (This story is from a 2017 issue of National Geographic.) Shadrack has spent the night, hands bound, dancing and pumping his arms in the air, revving up his growing adult energy for what he must face. This is the beginning of a long ritual that tests a young boy's worthiness and resolve in becoming a man. He must suffer physical and mental taunts from relatives, as well as having the guts of a cow smeared on his face and chest to prove that he can confront hardship. For many hours that evening, he is counseled by the elders about respecting his elders and women. After being allowed to sleep for two hours, Shadrack is awakened at 2 A.M. to undergo circumcision. He parades up the river with a large crowd of men and boys, his testosterone moving through his bloodstream. He now readies himself to face the moment: "The circumciser crouched at his groin. The operation was over in seconds...He would spend four days convalescing."

This ritual initiates a young adult Bukusu male into adulthood. From now on he is treated differently and given "a new set of patriarchal privileges," but also he is expected to fulfill a long list of adult responsibilities. Many traditional and modern cultures have similar initiation rites, although perhaps less intense. Ceremonies such as Bar-Mitzvah and Confirmation are rites of passage.

These rites represent the struggle or the obstacles to overcome in order to become an adult; what the adolescent needs to experience in order to change his thinking about the responsibilities of adulthood. Most men question the limits of their life at some point. This generally involves some struggle and suffering, and if faced with courage, it can benefit a man in his quest for a fuller life. This is another level of initiation—from being an adult to becoming the kind of adult you want to be.

Perhaps it is time to create some new rituals for ourselves. We can find ways to mark our transitions from "the way it's always been" to the way we have chosen.

— 3 —

BELIEF AND THE CONTEMPORARY MAN

All of our thoughts and actions are based on the way we experience and perceive the world.

Beliefs are conceptions of what life is about based on our sensory and intellectual experiences, and how we integrate them. Our beliefs form the basis of how we see life to be, how we translate those perceptions into action, and what ethical principles toward self and others we decide to live by. Besides our own direct experience, we learn from important others. For example, we are influenced initially by the perceptions of our parents and the society in which we live. These values are transmitted through the generations over time to become part of the fabric of the culture and the basis of how we see the world.

Our beliefs play themselves out in every area of life, including how we construct our physical world and its purpose, the mental and emotional concepts we adhere to, and the spiritual tenets we live by in order to explain the unexplainable. Our beliefs permeate all of our individual and social interactions, and they create the moral foundation for how we live.

SOMETIMES CHANGE DOESN'T COME EASY

He was of average height, sturdily built, with a gifted intellect. He spoke freely and eloquently in front of crowds, and his ability to stir people with his passion and wisdom were the envy his colleagues, as well as of many of his curious and brilliant contemporaries. His ideas challenged people's thinking, causing not only controversy, but celebration of his creative genius. He was greatly respected, especially in his circle of influence, but despised by a certain powerful group, which was ultimately responsible for his eventual demise. The Italian physicist and astronomer, Galileo Galilei, who lived during the late 1500s and early 1600s, is one of the great figures of history, and yet a man who was persecuted and imprisoned for his beliefs.

Galileo is known as the father of observational astronomy. His greatest legacy was his scientific proof that the earth and the planets revolved around the sun (heliocentric). This thesis disrupted the commonly held belief at the time that the earth occupied the central place in the universe, with the sun revolving around it (geocentric). Some people continued to believe in the geocentric model. Many beliefs drew from religious and biblical conceptions of the world, which were not scientifically based. The Catholic Church was the major influence on people's lives and beliefs at the time.

The power of the religious belief system was rooted in the perception that it was the moral authority. Its authority was based on the assumption that religion held the truth. This belief system was black-and-white with no grey area. It left no room for any other systems of belief. The judgments were final, and people were punished, sometimes beaten or jailed, if they veered from its so-called truths.

When Galileo published his theories about the planets and the solar system, he was branded a heretic and summoned to Rome to answer to the Inquisition. The Inquisition, established around 1100 AD, consisted of clergy whose task it was to root out heretics, and punish anyone within the Catholic Church who did not live exactly by its teachings. The punishment ranged from wearing penitential garb to imprisonment (even life imprisonment). There were occasions when people were even put to death.

Galileo was a courageous man committed to his beliefs. But the pressures of being silenced and the potential consequence of life imprisonment weighed heavily on him.

Once in Rome, he faced Pope Urban. Galileo spoke up clearly about his treatise on the universe. The pope was angered by Galileo for daring to deviate from papal authority (according to the church the pope is infallible), and wound up giving him a severe warning. He was not to publish any further writings, or do anymore public speaking on the matter.

Eventually though, he was branded a heretic and sentenced to life imprisonment. He was put under house arrest in 1633 and died on January 8, 1642.

I include this story of Galileo to underscore the power of belief. Others may hold their beliefs over us and we may feel threatened when we assert our own beliefs. Think about it: Both Pope Urban and Galileo had very strong beliefs.

Living and standing up for your own beliefs gives meaning to how we interpret life and what is important to us. When powerful beliefs clash, we may have an opportunity to refine our own, or we may be dominated by the other. Here it is not the beliefs themselves but our relationship to them that makes the difference.

CHALLENGING BELIEF:

The prevailing beliefs in the sixteenth and seventeenth centuries were very rooted in the culture. They served as a kind of container and blueprint for the culture to measure its decisions and everyday choices. Beliefs and associated laws provide structure and safety, and they are necessary for any society to function effectively. But beliefs evolve because change is inevitable as we learn more about the world around us. As people develop their thinking through new experiences, various ideas rub up against the existing structure of thought and challenge it to expand.

Clearly, change can be difficult. But change also can be the result of natural, gradual processes where there exists a readiness to develop new ideas, and people are prepared for transition. Changes are, of course, more welcome if the potential benefit is clear. For example, my client Connie decided to work a part-time job three nights a week in order to bring in more income. This meant that her husband had to come home right after work in order to feed their daughter, bathe her, and get her ready for bed. The arrangement was an uncomfortable adjustment, but the reward of increased income made it easier for them to adjust to the change.

Change is not always for the better, at least directly. There is usually not a benefit in the death of a loved one or the loss of a job, for example. Creating meaning out of suffering and pain can be a helpful part of anyone's belief system. It reduces stress and transforms a potentially negative experience into one that can provide positive meaning.

Sometimes, new ideas can be scary, and when anxious, we tend to cling to the familiar. New ideas threaten the equilibrium, as was the case with Pope Urban. We see the consequences of stepping outside the lines when, in the hands of a dominant culture, beliefs are threatened. We also recognize the presence of a belief system that leaves no room for alternative systems to function. One unfortunate factor in many systems of thought is an intolerance for difference. History reveals to us numerous examples of religious and other forms of intolerance. Galileo was persecuted. His discoveries were a threat to current thinking. He was labeled an outcast. In him, we have a glimpse of the power of a commitment to a personal conviction. Belief has many facets and its expression is present in all aspects of life.

What are our beliefs as men and women as to how we interact and influence our culture now? What we believe will be at the core of our actions. Do we work on acting in concert with what we believe? Are our beliefs consistent with the worth and potential of the culture? Our beliefs are central to who we are. They give meaning to our thoughts and actions and help define how we live out our lives. Are they insular or are they open to new information?

BELIEVING IN OURSELVES

Central to accomplishing any task is the belief that one has the capability to do it. You can have all the ability in the world, but without the confidence and belief in yourself to reach your goal, it won't happen. Most of us have the ability or the potential to do almost anything we put our minds to. Everything we need is inside of us waiting to be tapped. Having faith in ourselves can nudge us forward and become the driving force for successful action.

Beliefs can be so powerful as sources of motivation, fueling how we live our lives and what's important to us. They propel us into action, moving the structure and form of what we perceive in our minds, and translating the meaning into concrete form.

Believing in something that has significance can fill our lives with meaning and purpose. It stirs our passions and motivates us to pursue our desired goals. Honoring our own freedom of choice can and must include honoring the freedom of choice of others. Our uniqueness can live right alongside the uniqueness of others.

The power of belief also rests in its personal meaning for the individual in the most trying of circumstances. Meaning gives one's life purpose and direction. It infuses it with a positive energy towards fulfillment. In his book, *Man's Search for Meaning*, Victor Frankl (1946) writes:

"We who lived in the concentration camps can remember the men who walked through the huts comforting others, giving away their last piece of bread. They may have been few in number, but they offer sufficient proof that everything can be taken from a man but one thing: the last of the human freedoms — to choose one's attitude in any given set of circumstances, to choose one's own way... There is nothing in the world, I venture to say, that so effectively helps one to survive even the worst conditions as the knowledge that there is a meaning in one's life."

Meaning makes everything in life worthwhile. It provides structure and organization to our actions and gives us a reason to get up in the morning. And it becomes especially significant to the individual when we can expand and connect with others who have similar beliefs.

Feeling satisfied with our lives is an important ingredient in being able to love ourselves. When we're basically happy with our lives, we can be open to giving and receiving. Believing in oneself is an act of love. Believing in another is an act of love. When someone believes in you, it feels good and gives you a boost in confidence. It is an empowering affirmation of one's capability and one's worth.

In living out our truth, we share our values with others. This happens, for example, when we pass on our values to our children, and provide a basic structure for them to view the world. We may teach them formally or by example. As crucial as our established values though is the need to impart to them the significance of being open to the new and the different, to the ever-unfolding revelations of life's complexities. Children will be able to do this if we teach them to respect and believe in themselves so that they can respect and believe in others. The core lesson is that while we may not always know what to do in every situation, we have faith in our own worth, in our ability to face the unknown, and in our capacity to work things out.

BELIEF IN SOMETHING GREATER: USING LIFE'S RESOURCES

Sometimes, faith in oneself isn't quite enough for some people, and people have to rely on the greater power around them for solutions. This might take the form of a belief in the wisdom of other people, through the accumulated knowledge of the written or spoken word. We may also look to tap into the unseen power of nature to help us engage our inner strengths. Some people have faith that this available energy is a spiritual energy that we may not see, but that we can feel; that it is an intelligent power that is present as a resource for all of us. People may refer to this energy as God, who, may be referred to as the essence of life and whose energy is found in all of us. Others believe this unseen energy is physical in nature and contains the basic energy generated by the buildup and breakdown of the various interactive energy transitions taking place continually in the world around us. Belief influences how and where this energy is focused, whether it be in the physical, mental, emotional, or spiritual realms. Where we focus our energy is where our power lies. Moving into this unseen dimension contains many unknown resources and possibilities for us to explore. The biological and physical sciences continue to discover the possibilities of using this energy personally, and for the good of humankind. Where science is limited, human beings must use their intuitive and experiential sense of life to cull their beliefs and direct their energy.

Many people believe that this energy can be harnessed, and used consciously by the mind to create change. Think of the creation of art, music, and poetry, the erection of buildings and the laying out of roads, and even the construction of many areas of the social order — all were first conceived in the minds of people, and then translated into physical form. It all starts in the imagination and the belief that what is conceived in the imagination can be realized from the mental movement of energy. What if we take this idea a step further? Can the mind affect the body directly? For example, we know that meditation can slow down bodily functions and relieve stress, and that even having a positive attitude (rather than a negative one) has a healthy effect on one's body. In this case, what is the role of belief in directing our energies? Some people can focus their energies directly and with firm belief and intense focus, can draw that energy to themselves and create positive movement in their lives.

No matter the source, this energy is available for all of us to explore, call it universal energy, God, The Great Spirit, or something else. We just need to learn to tap into it. This invisible component of life is what stretches and expands us and who we are, and even the possibility of who we can be.

This limitless energy permeates everything around us. It's all energy; making up all living things as well as inanimate objects, and seemingly moving ahead in some organized fashion. Spiritual believers see this energy as the seat of growth and creativity. What we believe this energy to be and how we interact with it forms the basis of how we live our lives, what kinds of decisions we make, and for our purpose here, what kind of men we are.

FLEXIBILITY AND LIMITED REALITY

To be adaptive to our ever-expanding knowledge of the world, it's important to maintain a certain amount of flexibility and openness in our views toward life. We must be able to push through the limitations of old understandings for a deeper witnessing of our current reality and the possibilities of who we can become. Obviously, the prevailing ideas in Galileo's time were limited in their scope. As we look back, we understand the workings of the planets and the universe in more dynamic ways now. And the future will look back at us and see our limitations! With the evolution of more powerful telescopes and other scientific endeavors, our knowledge of the universe has expanded. And it will continue to expand. Questioning and examining our perceptions can help us decide whether we would like to change or remain still.

Limited reality is not pierced so easily. Even though scientific study illuminates our understanding of natural phenomena, some people cling to the old perspectives. In other words, they stay with what they've always believed. Some people are committed to their beliefs and hold to the perceptions that support them. Others may fear change. Still others may not know how to change, even if they want to. How many of our own views may be seen as limited reality, especially with respect to our restricted views about men and women, and even toward our own narrow conception of ourselves and our worth as human beings?

Believing in oneself and developing one's abilities beyond the current state requires courage and conviction. Sometimes the impetus shows up accidentally and is a turning point of life. Christopher Reeve, known for his role as Superman in the movie series, was cut down at the height of his career after being thrown by a horse and paralyzed from the neck down. The doctors told him there was no hope for recovery. He experienced a lot of depression and hopelessness, and even had suicidal thoughts. About six months after the accident, he had a revelation and was determined to make his life meaningful. He wanted to learn to walk again. He believed in himself and the power of the mind and visualization. He struck out against the current thinking that no one who suffered a spinal injury could ever hope to walk again! He started by moving his pinky, and actually progressed to taking a step. He lived for nine years after his injury. His courage to challenge the limits of what humans can do can encourage other humans to go beyond their own limits. During this time, he continued acting and directing, while devoting his life to advocating for stem cell research, and the advancement of techniques to improve the treatment of spinal cord injuries. He believed in himself and the power to create change, and it happened.

Michael J. Fox offers us another example of someone believing in himself no matter what life tosses at you. A very successful actor on TV and in films, he contracted early onset Parkinson's disease at the age of twenty-nine. He spoke to David Letterman on the Late Show about his initial reactions to the diagnosis. "It was pretty scary. I was twenty-nine years old, so it was the last thing I expected to hear...I thought I'd hurt my shoulder doing some stunt because I had a twitch in my pinkie." At that time the doctor predicted he'd have ten years left to work. Almost thirty years later, he continues to act, and tirelessly fight for a cure for Parkinson's Disease.

Here is a man who could have seen this diagnosis as a disaster for his life. Instead, he found a meaning for this experience and turned it into a positive force not only for himself, but for the millions of people associated with The Michael J. Fox Foundation for Parkinson's Disease. His belief in himself and the determination to see this as a constructive opportunity has extended his work life and given his personal life an added focus and purpose. More recently, he was back in the hospital with a debilitating spinal issue. He admits to some very deep despair, which it seems "meaning" has brought him back from — again!

The broader in scope the beliefs, the more encompassing the possibility for openness and expansion. Here's an example of how belief can work against us or for us. We have a certain perspective or belief, for example, that people of a certain culture tend to be aggressive and insensitive by nature. Now, feel into this next statement: All cultures have their element of aggressive individuals, and there are many causes that might explain this behavior. The first statement makes an overall judgment of a group of people by generalizing about certain behaviors. This level of belief leaves little possibility for change and expansion. The second statement leaves room for the accumulation of further knowledge. This belief offers a broader base for integrating further information as we learn more about other people and ourselves. This way of seeing motivates us to expand our knowledge and engage our curiosity in understanding more rather than settling into one view. The first statement ensures stagnancy, whereas the second invites growth!

SHARING BELIEFS

What you believe, when shared by others, can magnify its powerful effect with those who may identify with it. It grows and becomes stronger. It can also serve to unify and support a group of people, allowing them to deepen their own sense of personal meaning.

Expressing a belief to others in an enthusiastic and open way may be an invitation for them to share in its thoughts, feelings, and actions. We see this work often in political speeches, for example. Such a communication is designed to attract people to its message and get them on board. Some listeners may agree and become empowered by the ideas (of course, others may reject them). But those who listen to them with openness and critical thought can be inspired or informed. A great message communicated can help people feel supported and as though they belong, and the belief may then be carried forward in a good way, open to expansion and modification.

Unfortunately, sometimes messages are delivered with the intention of controlling people's beliefs, controlling them. We can think back a few decades to Jim Jones or Charles Manson. They were charismatic men who used their ability to influence for destructive purposes. We think about the influence of Adolf Hitler. His intent was to expand the Aryan Nation at the expense of other nations and cultures. His beliefs were limited and rigid. They may have provided a sense of organization, appealing to some in German society suffering economically after World War I, but the system scapegoated anyone outside his narrow categories. His beliefs exerted a powerful influence on a nation looking for something and someone in whom to believe. Belief in oneself at the expense of others is not really belief, it is fear.

INFLUENCE AND NEED

One important dynamic of a growing belief then is the ability to influence people who have a need, who are vulnerable. Poverty and feelings of depression were pervasive in Germany after their defeat in World War

I. At that time the Weimar Government was weak in responding to the needs of the country, and Hitler saw this as his opportunity to add order and meaning for the German people (order and meaning as defined by him). He saw a vulnerability that made space for his maniacal ideas. He used his ability to motivate the people through his speeches and various propaganda. These two dynamics — people in need and the influence of a leader bent on his own power — were pivotal in the spread of his belief system.

On the other side, many spiritual and secular leaders have been able to share important beliefs that have given comfort and support to people in need of meaning. Their messages have uplifted and broadened rather than suppressed and narrowed. We can look into our own hearts as men to discover whether what we communicate — to our children, our partners, our friends, the world — is meant to bend reality to our own sense of weakness or encourage us and others to rise up in strength.

The objective world can be seen and interpreted in an endless variety of ways. How we perceive the world and believe it to be are important ingredients in how it will be for us and who we can become as we navigate it. "Do you see the glass half empty or half full?" This simple and familiar question is a good example of how taking a particular position can determine the quality or tone life will take. Belief is a central component in determining who we are, and why we do what we do. In this example, seeing through the positive lens will tend to infuse life with more hope and possibility, while a half-empty glass reflects the view of what is missing. The power of the mind to create meaning and give it a concrete form adds to the diversity and structure of life. What we believe gives structure to life — on a societal level and inside our homes. The force and power of belief greatly influences the thought, feelings, and behavior of who we are, and it plays a crucial role in who we believe we can be.

— 4 —

MEN IN RELATIONSHIP

The human body is made up of twelve main systems connected to each other and working together as an interdependent unit for one purpose, the highest functioning of the body. No one system could function alone. Each system relates to the others in a cooperative fashion. Just as a car engine needs all its component parts operating in a planned, systemic way, the body relies on a network. The various parts depend on each other. They belong together.

As human beings, we have a need to belong—to feel we are a part of something. Dr. Gregory Walton has been researching this theme of belonging for over a decade: "Belonging is primal, fundamental to our sense of happiness and well-being…Our interests, motivation, health and happiness are inextricably tied to the feeling that we belong to a greater community that may share our common interests and aspirations" (CNN Health, 5 Things newsletter, 6/1/2012). When we are a part of something greater, we can feel protected and connected to others who are "just like me." The feeling, "I'm not alone," brings a depth of solace. We all belong to units that are larger than us, whether it's a family, a job, a belief system, or a gender, and so on. The feeling of belonging is essential to us.

Being part of a group allows us to feel we have a place and are acknowledged for who we are. We have an identity. We exist. We're important. Being connected to one another in a relationship is not only natural, it can bring us joy and meaning. Relationships are an essential part of life for most of us, and they are reflected in both our work and our personal lives. Whether relating to people, reading a book, or cooking a meal, we are always in relationship to someone or something. It is important to understand and appreciate these connections if we want to be successful human beings. Good relationships occur when we can get our needs met through connected exchanges in which both sides benefit.

When we consistently negotiate the relationships in our lives successfully, we can grow and have some feeling of satisfaction. But interactions don't always flow smoothly, and an individual can become frustrated if a blockage continues without resolution. A meaningful link with others is central to a fulfilling life. Without that connection, we can feel cut-off and become isolated and feel like we don't belong. This link gives us the experience of feeling a part of something bigger, where we can learn to give and take in an effort to achieve a sense of balance.

MEET STEVE:

Steve is ninety-three years old and has some physical challenges, yet he walks (with the aid of a cane), still drives a car, and continues to be clear mentally. Because of his sharp wit and friendly demeanor, everyone likes him. Given this, you might think he has many solid contacts in his life, but the truth is that Steve is lonely. Several factors have contributed to his state. Most of his contemporaries have passed on, and his ability to adapt to changing ideas is very much challenged. When he found out I was a family therapist, we began to talk regularly. It was clear he had experienced much heartache, disappointment, and emotional abuse. His wife had emptied his bank account shortly before she passed away, and he hadn't spoken to his daughter in nine years. He would be so emotionally overwhelmed by feelings of anger and hurt, people would get an earful whenever they spent more than a few minutes with him. There were times he wanted to give up on life because the pain of the loneliness was so great.

We began to address the issues of why he was feeling so disconnected, and what it is he might be doing to put people off.

He agreed that he was complaining too much but he felt he "couldn't help it." He also agreed he needed a more effective way to deal with his feelings. First, we put him in contact with a local priest who came to visit a few times. Steve would prepare and focus on what he wanted to talk with him about. This helped him to control his impulsive communications and helped him to organize his topics more, even in his own mind. We were also able to reconnect Steve with his daughter. As an initial step, she agreed to take him grocery shopping on Sundays. This became a ritual, something to count on. In addition, one of the parishioners began to bring him breakfast on some mornings, which helped extend his social network a little more. Steve now understands that he can do something about his loneliness, and that there are parts of his situation he can resolve.

What Steve Learned: He began by acknowledging that he felt isolated and lonely, something he had hidden, especially from himself. He took responsibility for his part, acknowledging that people felt overwhelmed by his complaints, and he reached out for help. Empowered by knowing he could do something about his loneliness, he stayed open to old and new connections.

When pain is acknowledged and felt, it can be addressed. Many people live with the ache of disconnection. Some are keenly aware, while others seem unaware. Some are fearful and don't know what to do. Acknowledging feelings of isolation and admitting not knowing how to bridge the gap are the first steps in resolving those things. Finding meaning through relationships can make the difference at any stage of life.

CONNECTING THE DOTS

Relationships, like everything else, have gone through a metamorphosis over the past fifty years. What men and women are looking for in a relationship has undergone a corresponding shift. Prior to the 1960s, men and women tended to be looking for a companion who would contribute to a good-enough marriage. Qualities such as maturity, having a dependable character, and emotional stability were the measuring sticks. Therapist and relationship expert Esther Perel (2019) states: "Marriage was an economic institution in which you were given a partnership for life in terms of children and social status and succession and companionship." People didn't spend a lot of time looking for passion. Even in the early 1960s, 76 percent of women and 35 percent of men were willing to marry someone they didn't love. In the 1980s, people became interested in something different. Eighty-six percent of men and 91 percent of women wanted romantic love. By 2008, according to Damon Ashworth (2016), mutual love and attraction became the number one factor for both sexes.

What constitutes a good, functional relationship today? It's different for each person and each couple. We have no single definition anymore as we once did, and so we need to continue to incorporate broader and more diverse definitions of relationship including gay, lesbian and transgender. The current freedom to expand our perceptions of what constitutes a good relationship means we can shape how to define our connections. In his book, *The All or Nothing Marriage,* Eli Finkel identifies three marital models based on his historical perspective: pragmatic, love-based, and self-expressive. We don't need to choose one or the other but can borrow from each one depending on our goals and those of our partner.

Today, relationships can be fuller and deeper if we choose. We can even use the strengths of the older, practical models, such as stability or security, and combine them with our needs for intimacy and personal growth.

An important quality in achieving a successful relationship in this framework is spending sufficient time with each other. You only get out of something what you put into it. In this fast-paced culture time is precious and, if we want a successful relationship we have to invest the time in attending to it and gain the psychological resources to create it. Wouldn't you make the investment in any important project if you wanted it to be successful?

Still, certain timeless qualities and some useful ways of interacting seem to facilitate positive connection.

One of the most basic elements of a working relationship is trust. You can't have any kind of effective exchange between two people without believing or knowing that you will receive what you need. Trust develops when we consistently receive what we need and when we give to the other our honesty and truth in return for what they need. When we don't receive what we need, or we experience an inconsistency in its delivery, we learn to distrust. This can lead to self-doubt. A person grows and thrives in an atmosphere of acceptance and a felt sense of personal value. A functional and trusting relationship is built on a base of honesty and truth — not on images or lies. Truth-telling begets trust and believability. When one can be sincere and truthful, it can very often invite honesty in the other. Trust and honesty can lead to a solid connection, and maintain it once it is established.

Another important element of any relationship is effective communication. This means being able to express one's ideas and feelings in a way that meaningfully connects to the other person's feelings and ideas. Our feelings are a main indicator of our involvement with life. Because of past conditioning and lack of opportunities for developing the feeling side, many men have difficulty expressing emotions. Because men have not historically been encouraged to develop their emotions, some may not even be aware of the existence of their feelings. This keeps them from coming into contact with and sharing in an important part of life's experience. A large part of life is a sensory and emotional experience.

When you have difficulty accessing that piece in yourself, you miss some of the grit and felt sense of your interactions. You may have difficulty empathizing and even communicating with others, and when you're not able to connect in this way, it may threaten your sense of belonging as well as the sense of acceptance on the part of the other.

PHYSICAL AND SOCIAL INFLUENCES AFFECTING RELATIONSHIP:

As outlined in Chapter 2, boys and girls come into this world with certain biological predispositions and strengths. These predispositions prime both sexes for certain unique, but flexible developmental patterns. The emergence of the various organ systems in the embryos of each sex is similar but not the same. We can imagine how some of the differences affect communications later on in life. As mentioned, females hear better at birth at the higher frequencies than males. These frequencies are connected to the speech centers of the brain. This could explain why girls generally may speak earlier than do boys. Also, in boys the development of the amygdala doesn't initially connect well to the verbal centers. Again, such genetic components are not determinant but they contribute to the unique experience of emotions between partners.

As time goes on, societal influences contribute a great deal to children's ideas about themselves. Boys are expected to be independent, not show weakness by crying and "being emotional." Girls are generally more socially oriented, and are encouraged to talk with someone when resolving problems. This early emphasis on independence in boys and a more social orientation with girls can be the result of early developmental programming of each sex. Of course, the unfolding genetic differences in the growth of the brain of boys and girls can also be seen as a predisposition in this direction.

With the assumption that boys can and should take care of themselves, the separation from the mother tends to be earlier than boys need. The expectation is that they don't need the same emotional support as girls

(Gilligan, 1982). In fact, they do need as much support as girls do, but because showing such need would be seen as a weakness, boys suppress it. There exists a double standard for many boys: Be sensitive, but don't show any emotions! They're in a bind. Sax (2017) explains, "Boys suffer silently inside from a confusing sense of isolation and despair. Feeling ashamed of this vulnerability, they mask their emotions, and ultimately their true selves. The unnecessary discrimination can cause many boys to feel alone, helpless and fearful." If this lack of being able to connect continues, the boy misses one of the most important experiences of an emotional bond: being known and understood by another person. Many boys feel stuck in this isolation with no language to express themselves.

Family therapist Terrence Real (1997), who has been working with men's development for over 20 years, says that this isolation and denial of men's need for intimacy and care-taking has left them with a basic feeling of shame and inferiority. Shame is a potent experience and many men cover it with feelings of grandiosity to feel better momentarily. Living in a patriarchal society, these vulnerabilities are glossed over and the man is protected from facing this part of himself. Terrence Real works to confront the inferiority by gaining a therapeutic alliance with the person and helping him to take responsibility for these feelings. When they can accept their shame and those lost parts of themselves, they begin to soften.

Can a man's partner or spouse help him to grow in his emotional development? In the end, this is usually one of the primary relationships in his life. Why not explore its strengths, and use the support of his partner? The partner needs to be careful though. In the zeal to help, the partner may be complicating his growth by getting their own emotional patterns mixed up with the efforts to help the other to change. In a 2018 online interview, Esther Perel stated that it's important to understand these spousal interactions and that there are no simple answers to how a woman can support a man in making changes. Perel says: "It's multi-layered. For example, a woman may want a man to change but be terrified by his vulnerability. Or, in order to help, feels she has to talk for him, or that she can say it better or faster than he can. She may even resent having to talk for him. Unless she's aware, these responses might tend to make her become more enmeshed with him and not support change." She goes on to say: "A more helpful approach overall is usually to just sit back and watch him. Support him, but let him do it." A man needs to be nurtured and heard, but he must come to change himself. Listening is a very productive process. When you listen, you allow the other person to feel heard, validated, and it encourages further expression. Reflect back his feelings to him. It is important in the long run that he feel challenged to look inside at how he's been protecting himself, and what his resources are. So, if you are a man reading this book, now you know what to ask for. If you are a woman, perhaps you understand better what could be helpful.

Perel (2018) explains that for a man to have a better relationship we have to help him deal with his issues of shame and inferiority, that the measure of happiness for a man is in his relationship and not in his curriculum vitae. To support this, she references the Harvard Longitudinal Study of Adult Development (Ted talks, Robert Waldinger). This is one of the longest studies of adults in existence. It followed 724 men over seventy-five years and found that good relationships keep most men happier and healthier.

MEET CHRIS:

Chris is a twenty-nine-year-old single male who had been feeling tremendous anxiety over the past month. The trigger for this feeling was that he had just broken up with a woman after being together for a year and he felt completely unglued. Out of desperation, he began taking an antidepressant, which was giving him headaches. He wanted to get to the bottom of his problems. He explained, "I'm tired of feeling this way." Having come to the realization that he had to stop blaming his parents for his problems, he appeared ready to make some real changes. Taking responsibility for oneself can be the first step.

I had seen Chris with his mother and younger brother twenty years earlier right after his parent's divorce. We remembered each other. His father, addicted to prescription drugs, saw his sons periodically over the years, but was mostly self-absorbed. His mother loved her boys and would do anything to help them adjust. Chris complained that she was always too critical of him, and that her expectations of him around being independent and caring for himself put a lot of pressure on him. She had been burdened with problems in her own family of origin, with a father who was emotionally distant from her and her sister, but a mother she was close to.

Chris felt confused most of his life, desperately wanting a relationship with his father, but his father would wind up taking advantage of Chris at every turn. Right now, Chris wanted this woman back in his life, and he was pursuing her constantly. As often happens when a person is pressured, the woman grew more distant. He was desperate for her attention but he was blind to his feelings. He could feel the anger and frustration, but he couldn't feel the sadness and hurt.

When we talked about those feelings, he agreed they must be somewhere inside, but he couldn't feel them. I explained that it was natural to have trouble processing certain feelings, especially ones that feel threatening. I assured him that his body held the truth and that it had been caring for him and protecting him from the pain this whole time. I explained that he had been holding these feelings for a long time and that it wasn't helping him anymore. I pointed out that he was stronger now and he deserved to feel his truth. He burst out into tears and began to release his long-neglected feelings that he had pushed down for so many years — feelings of hurt, loss, and abandonment.

What Chris Learned: Chris' breakthrough initiated new steps for him. He stopped pursuing his former girlfriend and began looking into the feeling he harbored about his dad. He found the courage to interrupt the negative patterns and instead examine its source, going deeper and breaking a cycle of pain. He took responsibility for his issues, rather than blaming his parents. In taking the initiative now, he was able to draw a boundary with his dad, limiting his contacts rather than feeling powerless and waiting for him to change.

This is one example of how men sometimes cover their vulnerable feelings with the one thing they think they're allowed to feel: anger. Chris enabled himself to feel his vulnerability and the buried feelings and needs that kept him from being a fuller man. He moved out of isolation and gave himself a language with which to express his inner world.

Everyone is unique. People respond to change in their own ways and their own time. Every person can decide what kind of changes to make for themselves, and what kinds of relationships to have in their lives. It's important to make it safe for people to consider change. People protect themselves when they feel threatened and tend not to want to take action when they are anxious. Creating a safe environment to see a fearful encounter in a new way can be an experience that is more acceptable. Instead of perceiving emotional expression as threats, they can be seen as a source of nurturance and support. If one man can open up to another in an honest and supportive way, he can make it safe to reciprocate.

MEET CHARLES:

Charles and his wife both work full-time jobs and share the pressures of raising three children. Charles is under tremendous stress at his job, and has many responsibilities in and outside of the home. Like most traditional men, he normally tends to distance himself from his emotions and winds up holding them inside. When he came to me this time, he let it all out. He complained about work and his wife. I listened to him and validated his feelings without judgment. As he finished, he suddenly realized that his wife had always been a resource for him. When I asked how she had been a resource, he responded that they had an agreement that they would always go to each other no matter what pressures they were under. "She was always a place of comfort for me," he said. When

I wondered what made him forget, he stated, "I was afraid she would be disappointed." After our conversation, he decided to turn to her — rather than away from her. In talking it out, and having someone listen without agenda, he found his own solution.

What Charles Learned: This may seem like a simple story, but it illustrates a very important process. It represents a successful way one man moved from isolation and despair to connection and relief. Rather than being threatened by his own feelings, he risked opening up and actually experiencing his vulnerability around feeling weak and imperfect. In doing this, he realized that these moments could be experienced as empowering to him. A sense of personal empowerment often leads to finding the help one really needs. In this case, Charles saw how important trust and his willingness to communicate with his wife were to him. He turned to his relationship as his resource. When we feel anxious and under pressure, we sometimes forget that our greatest resources are within reach.

LISTENING IS COMMUNICATION

Another often underestimated but central quality of a successful relationship is the art of listening. We usually focus on the importance of how we feel toward the other person or how we would like to act or what we want to say next. If you want to understand what the other person is feeling, you have to listen. Put yourself in their shoes. Many men are left-brained and in trying to help someone, and with all the goodwill in the world, they wind up giving advice. Sometimes giving someone good advice can be helpful, but feeling heard and validated often is the most powerful support. Listening to another without judgment can go a long way. Listening also forces us out of our tendency to make assumptions, or color over someone's point of view with our own. Doesn't it feel good when you know that someone is just focused on you and paying attention to what you say? It is so powerful to feel that what you have to say is important. This form of communication strengthens connections. It's important for each of us to connect our own dots with regard to what we want in a relationship.

THE IMPORTANCE OF TOUCH

Today, touch often has a very negative connotation in our society, too often being associated with physical and emotional mistreatment of one person by another. Because of our awareness of and sensitivity toward abusive adults, the healthy and crucial experience of trust, which initially begins between parent and child, is often very distorted. The experience of healthy trust, of which touch is an essential part, is critical in the bonding process. Understanding this, and not letting the exploitive and abusive aspects of touch encroach on this life-giving process is important. Touch can engender trust, one of the basic qualities for any person in building an effective relationship. Of course, in this moment, the idea of touch is influenced by the reality of COVID. Still, the acknowledgment of its importance helps us stay alert to safe opportunities and creative solutions.

The importance of physical touch in natal development was first highlighted in experiments after World War II from the early work of Harry Harlow studying primates and the work of John Bowlby and Renee Spitz working with orphans after World War II (February 1988, NY Times, "The Experience of Touch: Research Points to a Critical Role"). These observations involved distinguishing between specific chemicals released by the impact and experience of touch, and the absence of these chemicals when babies were left alone. The presence of these chemicals seemed to account for the children's ability to thrive. The "no touch" babies failed to thrive. Some even died.

Research on the importance of touch reached a high point in the 1990s. Tiffany Field of the University of Miami's School of Medicine (2018, November, Greater Good Magazine) has been studying touch for more than forty years. One of her studies involved pre-term newborns. They found that newborns who had three 15-minute touch therapy sessions per day for five to ten days gained 47 percent more body weight than those who didn't receive the therapy. Another result from her research was that massage actually increases natural killer cells, which are frontline defenses in our immune systems. These cells kill viruses and bacteria. Stress produces cortisol, which kills these natural killer cells. Reducing stress reduces cortisol and strengthens the immune system. In "Physiology and Behavior" (2003) Darlene Francis and Michael Meaney reported that the baby rats whose mothers licked and groomed them grew up calmer and more resilient to stress (stronger immune systems) than when they grew up without.

From a physiological standpoint, touch stimulates and soothes the vagus nerve, which runs the length of the body from the brain down into the gut. It is one of the most important nerves in the body as it is connected to heart function and blood pressure as well as gut and lung function. When the vagus nerve is calm and relaxed, body function improves in these important and critical areas.

Touch shows up in all areas of our lives. Handshakes serve to indicate welcome, conveying many non-verbal feelings of openness. Hugging carries meanings of comfort, love and support. We non-verbally communicate our feelings to our pets, and they to us through touch. In sports, emotions are expressed in physical contact from "high fives" to tackling. Even the touch of the fabric — silk, velvet, cotton, wool — creates sensations, including comfort, safety, warmth, and sensuality.

We are, of course, aware of inappropriate touch in various contexts of normal life. We are more aware of it now than we were even just a couple of decades ago. What was once deemed acceptable by some is now being called out and examined. With the recent exposure of powerful men who have been abusing and violating the personal boundaries of women and children, society has become sensitized to a basic abuse of power. We as a society can no longer turn a blind eye to the distortions in relationships with regard to power, sex, domination, and abuse. The

#MeToo movement has offered a way for men and women to confront the issue together.

The pandemic (COVID-19) has challenged the whole notion of physical touch and social closeness. Society is at a critical juncture with the spread of highly communicable diseases and physical proximity. Depending on effective diagnostic tools and eventual protective vaccines, the hope is to return to most of our present customs and way of life once the virus has been contained. But facing this pandemic, is a new experience, and there are no precedents for addressing it. One thing we know is that we are not going *back* (that's magical thinking); we must figure out how to move forward. Perhaps the Japanese bow will replace the handshake and we will "feel" touch in a new way.

COVID places our society in a very uncertain position. Being unsure of the nature of this virus and its capabilities, society is faced with reshaping present methods of social interaction and current practices regarding touch. This is just one part, of course, not even factoring in the painful effects of the pandemic on our local economics and global economies, as well as the fortification and retooling of our medical practices.

Over time, civilizations have had to contend with various forms of disruption whether natural or human-made in origin. These factors challenge a society to change and adapt, using all of its resources in service to its members. This is very consistent not just with the survival of the species but its will to flourish.

As discussed earlier, men already have a history of maintaining physical and emotional distance when it comes to feelings: "Don't show your emotions."

"Only babies cry." "Real men don't show weakness." "You're acting like a girl!" This traditional view may make learning to touch and express sensitivity appropriately challenging, but this is not an excuse. Understanding it, makes changing it an imperative. And, in little ways, many men are beginning to take hold of the importance of sensitivity and respect as central to relationship. When my first child was born, my wife contracted an infection and couldn't nurse the baby for the first couple of days. I was asked if I wanted to come to the hospital and hold our baby and nurse him. I was a little surprised and anxious at first, but I came into the hospital for the first few days, sat in a rocking chair, and fed and rocked our child. It turned out to be an incredible experience for me. As I rocked and sang to our son, he began sinking into me, and that feeling of unity was so engulfing that I didn't want to give him back to the nurse.

In thinking about the importance of touch, I recall an experience with my own father. I grew up in the 1960s and the early 1970s when society was undergoing tremendous change. Most of us were learning to express our feelings, especially as men. One day, I came home from college and as I came through the door, I hugged my mother, as usual. Approaching my father, I decided that rather than shake his hand, I was going to hug him. I don't know what I was thinking, or if I was thinking at all! I don't know whether I was trying to shock him, or I wanted to impress him with how different I had become. As I put my arms around him, I could feel his body stiffen. He pulled back so much that I almost fell into him! I could feel the awkwardness between us, but I kept going and even wound up kissing him on the cheek. This was the beginning of a breakthrough.

As time went on, it became easier to express physical affection until one day, as I went to kiss him, he kissed me — on the lips! It was my turn to feel awkward and hesitant. This had gone further than expected. The whole process turned out to be so positive, though. We were breaking down the awkwardness of the physical contact between us. Why can't men kiss each other? I didn't know it at the time, but it was one of a series of initial steps for me in facing my own fears of being "open" to others. Many other experiences would present themselves to me in the future that would challenge me to be transparent with the people who mattered. The experience with my father gave me something to build on!

Touch is an essential experience in any relationship. We can communicate our feelings about ourselves and our experience of the world. Valuing touch in a way that fosters understanding and respect, enriches the connection between people and enhances the quality of any relationship.

PRACTICING WHAT WE PREACH

How can we as men learn to trust our feelings and move toward more effective connection in our relationships? Here are six steps along the burgeoning path as we seek help ourselves and support others:

1. We have already mentioned the importance of creating a safe environment so men can feel comfortable and feel less threatened about making more conscious choices to expand their relationship skills. We can reduce self-criticism and practice being non-judgmental so that opening up to change feels safer and more possible.
2. We have to be ready to make the changes. This includes clearing any blockages from past learnings if they are hampering our movement. We can then confront some of the myths about men not being able to handle emotions, or equating vulnerability with weakness — ideas that took root in previous generations and are no longer relevant or useful.
3. We have to expose ourselves to new ideas about ourselves as men. Developing a curiosity about how other men are living their lives can expand our ideas about who we can be. We can seek out mentors to help us.
4. As fathers, we must give our sons the attention they need to explore their own emotions or teach them what it might take to relate to others more effectively. After all, we learn more about ourselves as we teach others.

5. We can read articles or books about men and relationships to expand our ideas about what's possible, practical, and inspirational.

6. Men's groups (or mixed groups) provide forums of exchange in which we can learn to understand what our partners want and need, and what we ourselves want and need.

Ultimately, it could be said that the most important relationship is with ourselves. We are only responsible for ourselves. If we love and respect ourselves enough, we can become happier, more connected human beings.

— 5 —

MEN AND THE NEW FATHERHOOD

Parenting has been a crucial element in the development and sustenance of life since the beginning of time. You would think there could be nothing new! Methods have been passed through the generations. They differ with each culture and each individual. Most people want their progeny to be happy and productive, and this is accomplished in many different ways. Expanding our consciousness of what's possible in becoming more effective parents allows us to make more informed choices about raising our kids in the current social climate. It also allows us to fine-tune our approaches to helping them to develop to their full potential.

This is the spirit of the new fatherhood: For each man to have the opportunity to reach a deeper, more mature level of parenting, becoming consciously aware of meeting needs and potentials that previously were left unmet. Men need to be more open to achieving a better balance in working with women more cooperatively. Rather than relying on using force to achieve their ends, men can become empowered to be conscious and aware of their true inner strength — able to support themselves and their partners to be the best parents they can be.

Over the past number of years, the viability of men's roles has been questioned by many in our society. This has only highlighted the lack of development in the areas of interpersonal communication and men's role in the family as fathers. Many women and men have questioned not only the relevance of the father, but some wonder about the importance of men in general. In the 2010 summer issue of the Atlantic Monthly, Hanna Rosin heralded: "The End of Men." A decade earlier, Susan Faludi (1999) put the decline of men in a more psycho-social context: "Men feel less triumphal, less powerful and less confident in making a living than their father's generation." She goes on to say that the previous generation valued loyalty and team play, and today we live with a "competitive individualism" revolving around who has the most, the best, the biggest and the fastest. The notion of working together cooperatively with our partners in support of a common goal as parents is sometimes lost in the transition. No wonder. Some 20 years later, the sense of the father's role in the family is still very fuzzy. Are the values and image of ourselves as men even less clear now?

Besides the evolution of social structures stemming from the change of moral values and the advances of women in their own right, some men continue to flounder. Many contemporary men are unable to settle into a meaningful role that feels important. Part of the issue is we seem as a society to emphasize status and appearance over substance. Society places such a high value on appearance and how things look that men can find it more difficult to connect to their deeper selves, which is exactly what is being called for. The development of a society has its own needs depending on the particular culture and time and place in history. These evolving needs create opportunities for people to fill new roles. As mentioned earlier, for example, the factories required workers to support the war effort during World War II, and the lack of available men created opportunities for women to work outside the home. This became one factor in women beginning to imagine something different for themselves. What openings exist in our culture today for men to imagine something different for themselves? Some men feel lost, some confused, but a large number of men are rising up to meet the challenge of being fathers who can make a difference. Amidst all the negativity, some research has highlighted qualities that distinguish their unique contribution to the life of the family.

HIS PRESENCE MATTERS

According to the US Census Bureau, 19.7 million children, more than 24 percent, live without a father in the home. That's almost a quarter of children who do not have fathers living with them for whatever reason. Consequently, we can surmise that the absence of the father is a relevant variable when we consider many of the social issues facing America today. A study resulting from a series of surveys conducted by the National Fatherhood Initiative (2017) found that nine out of ten parents believe there's a father-absent crisis in America. This study also noted that when fathers are involved, children are more well-adjusted socially and have fewer drug and alcohol abuse issues. In families without fathers, there is a four times greater risk of poverty, seven times greater likelihood of a child becoming pregnant as a teen, and a two times greater risk of a child dropping out of high school (National Fatherhood Initiative, Fatherhood in Crisis, Source: 2017, US Census Bureau).

A father's involvement in the family begins with a presence, a physical and emotional presence in the child's life. Even if he can't be available regularly because of his life circumstances, consistent contact is crucial to a viable relationship. In a study (Howard, Burke, Borkowski & Whitman, 2006) exploring father involvement, which followed 134 children born of adolescent mothers for the first ten years of their lives, researchers found that:

"…father-child contact was associated with better socio-emotional and academic functioning. The results indicated that children with involved fathers experienced fewer behavioral problems and scored higher on reading achievement tests. This study showed the significance of the role of fathers in the lives of at-risk children, and even true in the case of non-resident fathers."

Warren Farrell, PhD, spent more than a decade studying why children who have contact with their fathers do so well. He reported: "We are 100 percent certain that children do better in twenty-six different areas when they grow up in intact families. Children clearly pay a price when their fathers walk away or mothers keep dads away" (April 2017, First Things First, "Why Fathers Matter"). He notes that in a study of Black infants, the more interaction they had with their fathers, the higher their mental competence and psychomotor functioning was by the age of six months. William Jeynes and his colleagues (2018) present his recent meta-analysis of thirty-four studies regarding the unique role fathers play in childrearing. The meta-analysis included 37,300 subjects. His team defined the following: "Unique fatherhood contribution as paternal monitoring, involvement and child-rearing activities that can be distinguished from activities taken by the mother, another guardian, relative or caregiver." (July 5, 2018, National Fatherhood Initiative, The Father Factor, First Things First: Do fathers really make a difference?) In an article from The Atlantic (July 14, 2013, Wilcox, W. Bradford, The Distinct Positive Impact of a Good Dad) the following were identified as areas where fathers tend to make distinctive contributions:

1. The power of play — "The father's hallmark style of interaction is physical play that is characterized by arousal, excitement, and unpredictability." It involves movement, action and touch, all of which are essential to good connection. Action and movement are more historically connected with men.
2. Encouraging risk — Taking risks encourages the child to embrace challenges and be independent. Safety and security have to be ensured.
3. Protection — Shielding children from possible threats from the larger environment.
4. Discipline — The father's approach differs from the mother's discipline in the sense that it's firmer. In a longitudinal study of seventeen stay-at-home fathers, Kyle Pruett and psychologist Marsha Kline Pruett agree: "Fathers tend to be more willing than

mothers to confront their children and enforce discipline leaving their children with the impression that they in fact have more authority." In this same sense, fathers are also usually firmer about enforcing boundaries. Having boundaries is essential in developing your own individuality and respecting the needs and rights of others.

Kenneth Braswell, Executive Director of Fathers Incorporated (July 2017, First Things First, "Dealing with Anger from Having an Absent Father") says: "I am a Black man whose pent-up rage for my absent father drove me to do what I believed to be the right thing, for the right reason and with the right justification. Then I found out it was all wrong. Research agrees that there are hundreds of thousands of boys and men in America harboring pain and anger as a result of father absence." He goes on to say, "The more anger towards the past that I carry in my heart, the less capable I am of loving in the present."

WHY MEN LEAVE

Oprah Winfrey hosted a series of shows focusing on the topic of why men leave families. These men either had no fathers themselves, or their fathers were in and out of their lives. They had no real image of what a functional father would be, so they created a script in their minds of an ideal father and measured themselves against it. Most of the men wound up feeling unworthy and inadequate because they were never able to live up to this idealized image — and it had not been modeled for them. Since these men didn't have the language to communicate their feelings, and had no avenues to get the support they needed, they just withdrew from their families and distanced themselves through drugs and alcohol. When they expressed themselves openly and could connect to other men who felt the same way, they broke through their isolation and gained the support they needed. Once they found expression, connection, and support, they then had the opportunity to reconstruct their lives and to move ahead positively. One of the essential themes that came out of Oprah's series was the need to create more forums in which men can bridge that gap between themselves and others so that they can break free of their isolation.

Sometimes men don't stay because they find it challenging to maintain their place in the family and maintain a feeling of independence. Such a man may feel that if he commits himself to his child or children, he will give up his freedom to do as he pleases. They are afraid. And it is true, a commitment to another person involves taking responsibility for oneself. This man may even claim that it's a man's nature to be free, and he may fear that following through on commitment will threaten his masculine nature. This is a man who is not truly free, of course!

MY FATHER, MYSELF

A man's relationship with his own father is an important factor in determining his self-esteem. The power of connection between a father and his son facilitates a flow of information about how the son can see himself in that role. Every man reading this book had a father.

With respect to my own father, there were certain things I liked about him and other things I disliked. In my early adulthood, I had a clear interest in wanting to know him better. Like most men of that generation, he didn't talk much about his personal feelings. I would listen to stories about his family growing up and try to better understand who he really was aside from being my father.

In a graduate school training program, I was encouraged to explore the whole person of my father. Through a planned one-on-one visit, I devised a series of personal questions aimed at getting to know who he was as a man. What were his dreams as a young man? How did he relate to his own father, who had not been around for long periods of time? What was it like coming to this country as an immigrant with his mother and five sisters at the age of nine? I had to do this without my mother or anyone else present so the personal connection between my father and I could be maintained without distraction.

The experience was a productive one for me, and I believe for him as well. It got us to move beyond the role as my father and into some pieces of the man who struggled with real-life experiences, just as I had. I began to see pieces of myself. We were not so different. The things I disliked about him, I disliked about myself.

He was a traditional male at the core, and I thought of him as being very closed to any kind of change. But I slowly realized that he was the person who survived being uprooted from his country and who made a difficult adjustment to a new culture. He even taught my mother how to cook, and he encouraged my siblings and me to develop an effective work ethic. He wanted the same opportunities for his daughter that he did for his sons, and he encouraged us to do what we wanted with our lives. I embraced that part of him that wanted the best for his children regardless of gender, and I supported my own children in following their own desires. I can remember that while vacationing at the shore in the summer when my children were growing up, my daughter insisted on crabbing and fishing with the men and boys, despite the fact that the women were off doing more traditional "women's activities." I welcomed her. My father might have too.

On the other hand, like many men, he had a hard time expressing his emotions. Still, I learned from him some very important things about being a father: to allow your children to choose what makes them happy, the importance of spending time with your kids, and the value of being honest. It took me many years to understand who he really was.

I also learned about being a man from my mother. We had our conflicts when I was growing up but she was a very sensitive and intuitive person, and we spent a lot of time talking personally when I was an older adolescent. I learned the value of personal conversation, and that it was okay to have feelings and to be sensitive; that I could learn to trust my intuition about people. She taught me that I could be sensitive and emotional as a man. (I was referred to as the sensitive one among my siblings.)

My mother also could be judgmental and prejudiced, but as she grew older, she became more open and less rigid. When my mother was upset and unhappy with my father, she would criticize him. I would be very uncomfortable at these times. I was affected by many of these feelings and internalized some of the experiences, which, in turn, contributed to my self-criticism and feelings of not being good enough. I later learned that my mother's criticism of my father was oftentimes really about her own discomfort with herself. That insight helped me look more honestly at myself.

My mother did not work outside of the home until I was in middle school when she started to work as a school secretary to bring in more income. Besides the extra money, she derived great fulfillment from working outside the home, which I hadn't realized at that time. She too was a victim of a role she had to fit into, and I only noticed it as an older adult when my parents had an argument about where to live. She didn't want to leave her job and my father wanted to move away. She began the job in 1958 when most women stayed in the home. She expanded her own role when she had the opportunity to explore new options.

I've encouraged many people who want to know themselves better to spend time with a parent (especially one you may have conflicts with) to learn about who you are. Connecting and relating, rather than rejecting, can open new doors to yourself.

MEET CRAIG:

Craig is a thirty-year-old single man living at home with his parents. He had been feeling very anxious in general and was unwilling to interact with anyone with whom he was "uncomfortable." Even though he loved his job and felt very productive in his professional life, he was afraid to venture into anything new in his social life feeling fearful of being "trapped." Underneath, he experienced a great pressure to please everyone he met. His father was a successful businessperson, who was emotionally distant from others, even from the important people in his own life, especially his children. Craig was angry with his father and felt he was never there for him when he was growing up. He couldn't see having any kind of relationship with someone like him. He complained that all his relatives on that side of the family were the same, rigid and emotionally unexpressive. On the other hand, he felt a part of his mother and her family, despite their disorganization.

One day, we were speaking about what he wanted to accomplish for himself during his session. He said he wasn't sure, but that he wanted to stop feeling so anxious and be at peace. We agreed that physical exercise would help with some of his symptoms, but he had to find a way to move inward to experience his feelings despite his reluctance to interact with his father. I asked whether he could connect to anyone on his father's side of the family. (They were going to be gathering for the holidays.) He said he thought his older cousin had gone through a lot with her family and he would be interested to find out about her experiences. Maybe she knew something. We made a plan, including crafting questions for him to ask her related to his father.

When he did speak with her, he was "blown away" with the information about his family of which he was unaware. For example, he hadn't known the extent to which his father had been verbally and physically abused by his own father. Craig also felt a great deal of support from the bonding experience with his cousin and came away with a feeling of strength and validation as well as a new understanding of his father.

What Craig learned: He moved out of isolation and opened a channel of communication for himself. He got clarity on some of the limited perceptions he had of his father, including that his father had been abused as a child, which provided some context. This and other information led him to a softer stance toward his father and ignited a curiosity about moving toward his father rather than away from him.

Craig began to realize their many similarities, which eventually taught him more about himself, such as about his own rigidity and disconnect from people. Rather than complain and blame, the experience got him more interested in going inside of himself to make some changes. In this process, he began to expand his awareness of his complex emotional life, that feelings were layered and intertwined with other feelings. As a man, this was an important realization regarding the complexity and richness of emotions.

LET'S GET ORGANIZED

In this changing world, what it means to be an effective father differs with each man. It is not only certain valuable qualities that a man may embody that define him, but how he uses those abilities. A man may have a musical talent but it depends on how he uses it and to what extent he chooses to employ it that makes a difference in the world. We want to know ourselves and our abilities, and make the choice as to how we use them.

In the previous chapter, we spoke about some important traditional qualities of a relationship, such as trust, effective communication, listening, and emotional openness. And there are other important attributes that can strengthen the father's stance.

Part of being a helpful father means providing children with useful ways to organize themselves. Life has a way of becoming overwhelming at times and having a framework helps them make sense of an unpredictable world. A good framework can organize their thinking and reduce the anxiety that often accompanies feelings of overwhelm. They may not appreciate this framework all the time but the structure gives them a feeling of safety from their impulses and the world around them. Letting children know how you think, lets them know you care.

Effective structure is provided with clarity and compassion, along with a certain flexibility. Being flexible allows you to evaluate the effectiveness of a given framework. Is it in need of updating? Does it still hold, even if it could use a few tweaks? An effective structure has three pillars: It is well thought out; it is relevant to the child's safety and best interest; and, it is provided with compassion, firmness, and an emphasis on follow-through.

MEET SAM:

Sam, forty years old, came into therapy with lots of anxiety, anger, and lack of self-confidence. He was an only child, and went through school classified as "learning disabled." As a child, he was "hard to control" according to both parents and the school system, and ultimately he had to fend for himself. What he wanted most desperately was "to feel calmer and less overwhelmed." Growing up, there was little structure and no one knew how to show him how to slow down and help him to process his experiences.

In our work together, we focused on his impulsivity with regard to other people and events by learning to slow down and think before taking action. By stopping to take a few deep breaths before responding, or excusing himself from a room in order to calm down, he felt more in control. He saw the difference between reacting and responding. As he played more with learning to respond, his confidence grew. He realized he had had the capacity for self-regulation within him the whole time. More important, he felt good about himself. When he learned to build the structure he needed and wanted in his own life as an adult, he began to flourish.

What Sam Learned: He began to understand the nature of impulsivity and to find ways to pause between action and reaction. Being able to practice this, he discovered that this capacity wasn't outside of himself and beyond reach. This capacity was always within him, simply hidden from view. This discovery did wonders for his self-esteem and helped lower his anxiety and diffuse his anger.

I KNOW WHAT'S BEST

Reviewing and recalibrating our expectations of our children can be a source of strength in effective parenting. Are our hopes for them based on what we want for them? Or what we would want for ourselves? This is true especially with boys, who tend to be locked into the traditional stereotypes of what a boy should be. A boy can be labeled a sissy or less of a man if his choices are associated with some traditionally feminine activities. For example, Chris, age thirteen, loves to bake and do art projects. His father criticizes him at every turn. Fortunately, his mother and older brother encourage him and support his interests. It's important to show the willingness to expand our views, and value equally the unique strengths in our children.

MEET DANNY:

Danny is the father of Alex, fourteen, the middle of three children. Although generally quiet, usually keeping to himself, Alex did connect socially to a small group of friends in the school. His mother, Ellen, reported that he was angry and withdrawn at home and she thought he was depressed. Nevertheless, Alex loved music and the arts, and seemed to come out of himself when he started playing in a band. His parents felt somewhat conflicted. Although Alex seemed to enjoy the music, they had lots of concerns about the image of music and its connection to the drug culture.

Danny, a socially connected man in town, loved being involved in town activities and especially the athletic programs. Being a former athlete himself, he felt committed and had a great interest in helping to develop kids' athletic abilities. He had given lots of time and attention to the development of Alex's athletic skills over the years, and was eager to coach his son's baseball team.

We scheduled a session with Alex and his parents. Alex expressed little overtly, but he showed some anger and frustration. As I usually do, I split the session, having the whole family in attendance during the first half and seeing Alex for the remainder by himself. When I saw him alone, he verbalized his anger toward his parents. He explained: "They never listen to me. They think they know me and what's good for me... If it's not what they think, I can't do it! I don't want to play baseball this year, and they're forcing me!" Like many parents, they believed they were listening. They "heard" what he wanted to do, but felt they knew the best course for him to take. Surely this would be healthier for him and more in line with what Danny wanted for him. How many fathers have fixed notions about what their sons need? How can Alex begin to be heard and allowed to have his own interests?

During sessions over the next few weeks they learned to talk more candidly with one another. They began to reduce their judgments, listen a little better, and be more open to more useful and effective ways of resolving this blockage. One of the tasks that helped things shift was the parents' agreement to attend a "Battle of the Bands" in which Alex's band was entered. The parents were surprised by Alex's musical ability and the talent of the band in general. The parents' thinking began to change.

What Danny Learned: As a father, Danny has to allow Alex to develop his own unique qualities. He took a chance and stepped out of his own shoes and feelings by going to see his son in his own framework (music). Most important, Danny opened his heart and mind to realize and value that Alex has unique abilities and interests and that they are different from his — and that's okay.

DIVORCE: THE CHANGING ROLE OF THE FATHER

Divorce has always been a reality. There are many reasons why marriages end, and a variety of circumstances that surround each couple's experience. Why some relationships don't survive and others seem to thrive also varies. Although I will refer to certain marital issues in specific families, it is a given that there are myriad causes of marital conflict. Here I am concerned with the effect divorce has on family structure and function. In particular, how does it shake up the role of the father, and what are the effects on the children? Consistent with the theme of this book, the purpose is to see how innovative ideas to support parenting transitions can shape new, and more connected relationships between fathers and their children. Today, the divorce rate at present is 40 to 50 percent (February, 2018, American Psychological Association) and the ease with which the process can be completed has had an effect on family cohesiveness. The speed and ease with which couples can end their relationship can make is easy for people to avoid the task of processing feelings.

Divorce is a difficult family transition to negotiate, for both children and adults. What used to be a recognizable unit with which kids identified and felt safe no longer exists. When a shifting familial landscape occurs across the society, it poses challenges on a systemic level. It becomes a collective problem for the community, including how to manage an increasing number of children struggling to adjust. Parents must take responsibility. Fathers don't have to feel separate, or separate themselves from the family. Sometimes fathers may be afraid or ashamed, or too angry to take their responsibility for the family's well-being. A father needs to decide to care in order to be a proactive part of the divorce process. He has to honestly identify how it affects him first, and then he can better understand how it's affecting the children and step up appropriately.

Most men go through the divorce process flooded with various emotions and confusing thoughts that they have not learned how to feel and integrate. The course of events in itself is a major disruption in one's life, and can leave one feeling empty and disoriented. Feelings of shame, fear, and inferiority are easily triggered. To avoid these feelings many men bury themselves in their work. It is rare that one can really have a complete sense of what the experience is as it's happening. Even when it is over, some people stay protected, cut off from their own feelings. These feelings may be compensated for by a kind of grandiosity, being distant emotionally, or falling into substance abuse issues. Such responses serve to cover the pain temporarily.

The opposite response is to be as conscious as possible about what you're feeling — day-to-day, sometimes moment-to-moment. This way you can choose a path that with support can ensure that feelings can be expressed and processed among family members. Consciousness allows for growth and with the accumulation of self-knowledge comes opportunities to make mindful decisions. But people can get lost in the fast pace of life and the seeming negation of so much that once seemed important.

Of course, divorce can be a good thing because it can relieve situations that are no longer functional. Still, the pressure to resolve matters sometimes doesn't allow people the time and space to work out a good transition. It's important to remember that as we go through the process, we can discover what's really important to us. We may realize the need for a deeper connection with our children — or with our friends or our extended family members. Maybe all of the above. We may discover new strengths in ourselves. We will only find out if we have the courage to really feel into what we are going through.

When I was faced with divorce in my own life, I was scared…afraid of losing the dream I had about the life I wanted. It took me a couple of years to make this decision. I was afraid, and couldn't get away from my intrusive thoughts and feelings. I saw only limited possibilities open to me. When I finally left the house, I felt like I was on another planet. Everything was new, strange, and uncomfortable. I needed professional support as well as the support of the men's group to which I belonged. I didn't want to feel the upset and pain of being more responsible to myself, and I didn't want to be separated from my children. I decided I was going to be a better father and a better man. To be fully involved in the divorce process means to be present to yourself just as you are, the painful feelings as well as the new ones. Transitions of such magnitude include many moments of learning — for everyone.

The willingness to love through the pain and to appreciate the needs of the children even as you are keenly in touch with your own needs is central to remaining relevant as a father. To leave the marriage but not leave the family is an intricate process well worth the effort.

A father must be sensitive to what the children might be going through. He can do this by maintaining a physical and emotional connection with them so they feel cared about and feel part of the process. The progression of the divorce can be isolating, especially for fathers. If a man is emotionally isolated already, divorce can exacerbate the feeling. He can feel alone and his emotions can intensify with no outlet. Thus, it's especially important that he use his support systems — or discover some — at this juncture. Whether it be family or friends, a man needs to lean on others. Unfortunately, many men feel ashamed if they have to rely on others, and many have no idea how to do it. This goes back to the idea of rugged individualism. "Pull yourself up by the bootstraps" is the hackneyed phrase that reverberates. I felt embarrassed and ashamed to open to others at the beginning of my divorce. It was not until I decided to share my feelings with the men's group that I realized how good it felt to unload my pent-up emotions and receive support. We can do it for ourselves first, and, in so doing, teach our children the value of sharing their feelings.

It can be hard to slow down enough to attend to the deeper levels of what's happening. But as parents we are the ones in the position to take charge when there is chaos in our families. We need to have accountability. Again, this begins by respecting our children's feelings and using the power of our connection with them as guidance. In this way, we let them know that they are important in and of themselves, cornerstones of the family unit, and part of something bigger, no matter the twists and turns of family life. Their input and value are essential. It doesn't mean that they'll always get what they want, but that their emotions and ideas play an integral role to the ongoing life of the family and its success. Through us they learn to face challenges, and they have the chance to see that solutions are possible through relationship, dialogue, and a willingness to grow. We, as parents, can ensure that they have a voice and understand the importance of give-and-take in life. Even though the configuration of family life may shift, the growth and support it provides does not.

WHEN WHAT'S "REASONABLE" SEEMS IMPOSSIBLE

For various reasons, the seemingly healthy divorce approach may not be feasible for some families. Some parents may be so consumed by their own difficulties that they find it impossible to attend to their child's struggles. Other parents may not know how to effectively connect and speak with their children. Some fathers and mothers are great at connecting with their kids when things are going well but have a hard time when difficult situations present themselves. Many men don't feel it's their place to cause any more pain than is necessary and so become withdrawn. They may distance themselves from their kids because they are afraid of hurting their feelings or seeing them struggle. This type of distancing is in an effort to protect the children, but who's really being protected? Are these fathers really protecting themselves?

We can talk with our kids about divorce, but many men are not close enough to their own feelings to relate to their children and the variety of emotions their kids may experience: anger, sadness, guilt, fear of abandonment, over-responsibility, and more. Children have a thousand questions: Where will I live? Will I see you? How often? Do I have to leave my friends? Why is this happening? Am I responsible for what's happened? A father must be open and honest about such questions. To do this, he needs first to be open to his own feelings, and not be afraid to relate his own uncertainty. After all, who can children go to with their fears, confusing emotions, and conflicting sensitivities, if not the people who are charged with their care? It's a time when men can step up and not be afraid to feel what they feel with their children. It's a moment to be strong enough in oneself to affirm their children in their time of need. Strength doesn't preclude sadness or any other feeling. Strength is in acknowledgment.

SINGLE PARENTHOOD

Being a single parent, can put a strain on our children. Generating enough income often becomes more difficult, and creates an added demand on our time. One income isn't usually sufficient. And although it is ideal when both parents can contribute time and resources, it is not always possible. Many fathers don't uphold their responsibilities when it comes to support. Oftentimes, their view of support is based on a reactive position toward the former wife. There may be anger about the amount of alimony and child support mandated by the court, or fear that there isn't enough to go around.

This worry is felt not only financially, it is experienced with regard to our personal time. Just as our commitment to our children calls for something more from us, it is also important to attend to the balance of our needs so we make sure we get time for ourselves. Most women who serve as the custodial parent understand the time crunch of having to work and raise a family. As many men become more active in choosing to be custodial parents, they are beginning to realize the strain of trying to juggle parenting and work. With all the added pressure, it can be difficult to find that balance.

MEET LEO:

After his wife deserted the family, Leo had the responsibility of caring for their seven-year-old son. His mother and aunt offered to take care of his son but he was determined to do this himself. His job had been a shift work situation but he arranged a way to work permanently during the day while his son was at school. He would get him up and out in the morning, and he placed his son in an after-school program. Leo had lots of rough spots, but he loved his son and wanted to be an actively engaged father.

What Leo Learned: He taught himself that he could rise to the occasion, find the resources he needed, and take full advantage of the opportunity to be the kind of father he wanted to be!

MAKING TIME COUNT

Time may be money in some contexts, but it is worth more than money in a family. Giving and spending time is probably the most essential ingredient in building trust, especially when parents are divorced. If the mom has primary responsibility for childcare, the dad must be deliberate about spending time with the children. He must make the investment, if he is going to forge meaningful ongoing contact. Giving attention to how the time is allotted for visiting, and how that time is spent, adds to the feeling of security and richness of the contact, especially if the importance of the visit is discussed and appreciated by the father and child. The financial agreement between spouses should not be a concern for the child.

The matter of support must be honored and agreed upon as laid out in the divorce settlement. This is a bitter pill for some men because it is often associated with many resentments that have built up over the years. However, for the father this represents a responsibility and commitment to the children. The reliable father always shows up.

As the family structure alters, creating uncertainty and fear for the kids, many kids involve themselves in the interpersonal dynamics of divorce out of guilt or a misplaced sense of responsibility, and they often get themselves caught in the parental skirmishes. Some parents have poor boundaries, and involve their children in their conflicts. This is unfair to the child.

For the evolved man, keeping his children out of the dynamics of divorce is a clear purpose. He keeps the issues of marital conflict and financial support between he and his former partner while concentrating on spending quality time with his kids and being present for them.

Responsibility should not be a chore but a gift. This is the only good message for the children.

It often is not the case, of course. My client, Robert, for example, could not stand to be in the same room as his former wife. So, the way he chose to deal with his anger at her was to send messages to her through their eleven-year-old son, Ronnie. He would belittle her to their son and create emotional upheaval for him. Both parents eventually began using their son as a conduit for fighting with each other. Ronnie was stuck with a lot of confusing feelings and undue pressures. Unfortunately, such fathers (and mothers) are usually emotionally immature and selfish. They indulge themselves in their own concerns, and their behavior causes added stress for the children.

If the parents' relationship is acrimonious and out-of-control, how can their children get the support they need? The importance of identifying support systems to be on hand is critical in preserving family stability. For example, the grandparent or aunt or uncle can help balance the angry and confused feelings with more positive experiences for a child. It is not unusual for other relatives to step into unstable marital situations in order to support children.

MEET FULTON:

Fulton had watched as his adult daughter started connecting with people who were not on a healthy path. She and her husband had gotten involved in drugs through a group of mutual friends. They had been fighting constantly and their nine-year-old son and seven-year-old daughter were being caught in the skirmishes at home. No one outside really knew what was going on. Fulton would take the kids to his house a couple of times a week to help with homework and give them a place with some stability. On weekends, they would go on hikes or take trips to the park. Fulton protected the kids and provided them an alternative, calming experience. It meant a great deal to the children to have their grandfather step in. He was the positive alternative, representing a loving, supportive parental influence.

Eventually, partially through actions he took, Child Protective Services got involved and the children were temporarily placed with him. After the parents took part in a drug treatment program, the whole family wound up in counseling and things began to get sorted out. The importance of identifying support systems to kick in when necessary, including state agencies, can be critical in preserving or reestablishing family stability and the well-being of the children.

What the Family Learned: The grandfather stayed alert and offered his grandchildren a steady environment, and an alternative reality to that of the parents. He called in outside help when it became necessary, but remained open to the parents being able to change and reclaim their role as parents. The family learned that even when things fall apart there is the chance to come back together once help is enlisted and everyone takes responsibility.

Discordant parents need to be aware of the negative effect they're having on their children. Once they become aware, they must make a move to turn the tide. Becoming less preoccupied with their own issues, they can focus on the needs of their children.

In another case, William, whose own father was not in his life, had the responsibility of "fathering" Jimmy, his seven-year-old step-brother. William was just fourteen years old. When their mother divorced Jimmy's father, her work, and also her fighting with Jimmy's father and trying to untangle herself both emotionally and physically from him, distracted her from parenting. William took on the task of caring for his little brother. This weighed heavily on him, but he loved his brother and would do whatever he could to help his mom. This mother loved them both.

William's mother eventually realized she had enlisted his help with tasks that were not his. He was being parentified. Once she became aware of it, she decided to relieve him of some of the responsibility and she stepped into parenting Jimmy. Jimmy also began to learn to do certain things for himself.

Could things have been any different had the father been present? Yes, if the dad had stayed present to their sons even as he withdrew from his wife, William might not have seen himself as the "man of the house." A responsible step-father could also have shouldered some of the childrearing but only in full cooperation with their mother. Further, he would have to stay out of the conflict between the mother and her former husband, always respecting the parenting role of both parents.

MEET JORDAN AND MAUREEN:

Jordan and Maureen had been married for six years, and had a four-year-old daughter, Samantha. Jordan had been married twice before: Of the first marriage, he said, "She spent all the money." The second marriage lasted two or three months. He reported: "She was out all the time, and I got jealous!"

Jordan and Maureen had been fighting constantly and had decided to get a divorce. He accused her of being just like her mother and not caring about anybody. She felt he was not emotionally expressive and was critical of her independence. He was a police officer and loved his job. He had no problems sharing, "I would do anything for the guys at work!" Some men have difficulty with female energy and have a strong history of male bonding. Traditionally, we find this among many male police officers, firefighters, the military, etc. They are very faithful to each other and give unending support when needed.

Jordan and Maureen's arguments developed into loud confrontations and their daughter would cry and become very upset. Despite some initial urgings on my part, they could not control these outbursts.

After threatening to bring a domestic violence complaint against him, he became enraged, and responded by refusing to pay his share for a birthday party for Samantha. He took his anger out on their child.

At this point, I asked them if they would come into the office together, assuring them they could solve the problem of the recent escalation if they worked at it and put their daughter first. They finally understood that their uncontrolled anger was self-serving, and the one suffering the most was Samantha. They promised to stop fighting when the little girl was present, and to find ways to spend quality time with her.

Maureen alerted the pre-school of the situation about the pending divorce. She wanted Samantha to have the additional support. Trying to keep Jordan focused on himself and not Maureen, he continued meeting with me. He eventually realized his relationship with his own mother was overly close and dependent. He described his mom as his executor, for example, explaining: "She has always handled and paid all my bills!" It took a while, but he finally learned how this pattern played a role in his other relationships. His mom had always taken care of him. He realized this had some negative impact, and we worked to begin getting him to do more for himself in little ways. This initial insight mitigated some of his anger toward his wife, and helped him refocus more on himself, and on his already loving energy toward his daughter. The situation began to improve.

What Jordan and Maureen Learned: Once they realized just how much their self-absorption — indulging in loud arguments even when their young daughter was present — was hurting the daughter, things began to change. They faced the fact of their impact on her and began to take steps to shift their knee-jerk reactions. Maureen enlisted the help of Samantha's school to track her during the divorce. Jordan realized some deeply embedded patterns with his own mom might be undermining his sense of capacity in handling the situation more effectively. Together, they began to move out of the destructive interactive patterns and make space for positive parenting!

How does the increased physical and emotional distance of the non-custodial parent, who has not been responsible, affect the relationship with a child? Most of the time, this question involves the father. A divorce can be a turning point for many fathers. It is in itself a defining moment. It's a disruptive event in the life of the child, who struggles to make sense of the confusion, and the further the father is from taking responsibility, the more the child usually suffers. The distant father leaves no chance for himself or his child to process and heal. He has to make a choice. He has an opportunity to look inside himself, and perhaps even to his "dark side," where he must face and accept his own contribution to the relationship. He can take a good, hard look at himself using a balance of sensitivity and honesty in order to pause and consider how to move toward his children. This can happen with just about any man at this critical juncture. It's a chance to make a greater commitment to himself, and to facilitate continued connection with his kids. The process of taking responsibility likely starts off with much turmoil, maybe including blaming others, or perhaps even denying that there is a problem. If he can confront the pain and learn from it, he can transform it and make it a life-changing experience.

MEET THEODORE:

Theodore was a single father and the non-custodial parent of his two boys. On one occasion when the boys were visiting, Theodore had been play-wrestling with them, and tempers got out of hand. The oldest boy was hurt when Theodore lost his temper. When the boy returned home, the mother was appalled by the injuries. She reported the incident to Child Protective Services, and contacts between Theodore and the boys were suspended. He was then remanded to attend anger management training, as well as a weekly parenting group. This was in addition to meeting with me.

When all this happened, he was in shock, and his life was thrown into a tailspin. How had this happened? Wrestling with his eldest son had gotten out of control. He had let his own anger get the best of him.

As events began to unfold and the consequences of his actions began to hit home, he became more depressed. His anger bubbled up inside of him, but he couldn't express it. He loved the boys and was not prepared to lose contact with them. The boys were having a hard time without him as well. The relationship was damaged. The eldest son was riddled with guilt and both boys were experiencing high anxiety.

Theodore reached a crossroad. Was he going to fight these charges, or would he use this experience to learn more about himself? He decided on the latter, and to have a good, honest look at himself. In the process, he learned that his anger was okay to feel, and that he could learn to release it appropriately, and not hold it inside. He discovered its roots went all the way back to his own father and the cut-off from him that he experienced when his father divorced his mother and left the family. He experienced anger, guilt, and shame. This realization helped him to own his emotions and not act them out on others. In addition, he gained a lot of knowledge and support from the anger management group. The visits with the boys became more frequent and regular and more productive for all of them. Theodore reported: "The divorce and everything I went through with my sons has made me a better man and father."

What Theodore Learned: Rather than fight the accusations Theodore chose to explore the truth. This was a courageous act. How many men would choose not to look at themselves, but instead be distracted by the injustice or embarrassment of the incident? His openness allowed the boys' anger and feelings of guilt, anxiety, and sadness to be validated and all three to take a step toward healing. The boys learned that fathers can make mistakes and take responsibility. Theodore was able to see his anger in a broader context, connected to both past and present.

What happens when a man makes a solid connection with his child, and has other responsibilities that put demands on his time? Many men know the importance of being there for their kids, but have difficulty making it the main priority in light of the practical realities of work and daily stresses. The hustle and bustle of our present-day lives can convince us that it's necessary to put off the essential things even when we have a desire to be responsible fathers. It's important to bridge this gap with the emphasis on the quality of contacts, no matter the quantity. Generally, men who have realized the joy and satisfaction of a meaningful connection with their sons or daughters will do whatever it takes to be with them. The child will feel the genuineness of his presence. My own experience bears this out. Having to run my own business occupied lots of my time, and I didn't always make good decisions when it came to spending time with my kids. I gradually realized how important it was to be there when I could, and to make the time meaningful.

THE NEW FATHERHOOD UNFOLDING

Another characteristic of the new fatherhood is resilience. Resilience is an essential ingredient in effective parenting, especially following a divorce. The resilient man feels the pressures of the transition but has the ability to learn the lessons that come with it, and to bounce back to stay connected with the children in authentic ways.

The responsible father always shows up when he's needed. This man keeps his word and follows through with action. He realizes that being there for his partner and his children is one of his most important attributes. It speaks volumes, more than any words can say.

Connection is also strengthened just by physical presence. Many adolescents and adults I've worked with over the years have spoken painfully about their parents not being present at the various events they participated in as children. Not being present at recitals, sporting events, award ceremonies … this has an impact on young people that is remembered long into adulthood. They often carry these kinds of messages in their hearts: "I just wanted them to see me in the play!" "Other parents showed up!" "Maybe it wasn't a big deal, but it mattered to me!" Just showing up can be everything.

All children want to be recognized by the people who are important to them, especially their parents. It affirms their sense of self-worth when someone takes an interest. Sometimes, I would take time off from work to attend a game after school, or an award ceremony. Even when my kids were older and were embarrassed by their father being around, I'd go anyway. No matter how they felt, I wanted them to know how important they were to me.

Communicating your love and that you value them can take many forms. Being present for them in times of trouble is essential. We all make mistakes and run into situations when we need help. When our children have done something wrong, they need guidance in accepting their mistake and learning from it. They have to learn the benefits of their missteps. If they've been misunderstood in an interaction with their teacher or their peers, they need to learn to think it through for themselves. We can help them, not so much by telling them what to say or do, but by asking them questions so they can learn to question themselves and begin to see they are responsible for — and capable of — evaluating their own behavior.

Being there for them even if we disagree with them or are disappointed with their choices takes a certain amount of self-discipline on the part of a parent. This ability reflects a level of maturity (not always easy to access). Do I want to show my disappointment in them? How do I express my disagreement? Sometimes, it's important to express it, but always in a thoughtful way. There are two guidelines that I use. First, is it important to the situation for me to express my reaction? Second, if it is, how do I want to do it? What is most useful in the situation? Waiting until you make a more complete assessment and not reacting immediately is not only fair to everyone involved, but it shows the child you're interested in the truth and will take the time to get it. It's also a respectful way to treat the relationship. We teach our children by modeling a caring and loving approach. The resilient man bounces back from a divorce and from challenges with any other difficulties which interferes with his children's well-being.

Is there a difference for a father between raising a boy and raising a girl? A father should treat a girl with the same respect and have the same expectations for her that he has for his son. He needs to be aware of the sexual biases she will most certainly face as she develops into a woman. She should be reflected and supported for her intelligence, athleticism, her practical mind, in addition to whatever else is important to her as a growing individual.

The contemporary father needs to be aware of any tendencies he may have to direct either his son or his daughter to the life he thinks is appropriate, and encourage them to choose their own path. To whatever extent he employs this approach, it is always age appropriate in terms of ability and readiness to make choices. At any age, we encourage them to think out the situation and consider possible solutions.

There are times, of course, when decisions must be made by a parent. When children don't know what to do, and after discussion with them, a father can make a decision based on the best interest of the child and the appropriateness of the response to the situation.

There are many fathers out there who are making changes and giving the best to their kids. Parenting in this day and age demands a willingness to be present and involved. An evolved father has developed both his masculine (yang) and feminine (yin) qualities and uses them in the best interest of his children's development and growth. He also can show the courage in making changes for himself, continuing to be committed to teaching and living his meaning in life. He may be afraid at times, but his willingness to show his vulnerability and express his feelings will show his sons and daughters that fear is natural but not insurmountable. Today's father acknowledges his partner's gifts whether or not they remain married. He understands the value of cooperation.

— 6 —

MEN AND STRESS

STRESS

Stress is one of the central experiences of all living things. Stress comes with managing the life process of any given organism. It is the accumulation or buildup of physical and emotional energy in our daily encounters with life. Without release, this energy is felt as pressure. Ideally, this energy flows freely in the body, is processed by it, and is then released. We talked about the yin (female) and the yang (male) energy from Eastern medicine and how physical/emotional stresses cause blockages in the flow of energy through the body. Periodically, energy becomes congested as physical and emotional factors overwhelm the system. Here's an analogy: A river may flow unobstructed until it reaches a dam. When the dam is clogged, the water can't pass through as easily. Over time, the water may back up, the pressure building and building. It may seem as though the walls of the dam are going to break, or areas that had once been filled with water, dry up. It's a similar process in the body when the natural flow is interrupted.

The emotional experience in and of itself may threaten the system. Imagine, the adult man who experiences stress in caring for a sick parent. At some point, let's imagine he loses his job, and what's more, his child is facing challenges in school. Here, the accumulation of emotion — the stress of what is happening all around him — may slow down the ability for the body to process experience. Over time, this will compromise not only his ability to manage the specific stressors, but it will undermine the functioning of the whole system.

In addition to the daily build-up of tension, ways of dealing with stress can be passed down from our parents. The navigational tools may include both effective and ineffective strategies. We may learn from our families that when you become stressed, you turn to alcohol to calm the agitation. Or maybe our parents just shut down and refused to talk about stress. If this happens on a consistent basis, though the stress may seem to eventually pass, it actually just goes underground. And, of course, these particular tools cause their own problems in families. On the other hand, if your mother or father jogged or went to the gym when feeling under pressure, the blocked energy—even if not the source itself—could be released. Or, if your parents were able to talk and connect in times of stress, things could be right-sized and solutions might be found. Family history imprints an individual's patterns deeply. In other words, if you want to deal with your stress more effectively, it may be more difficult to change if you're stuck in a maladaptive pattern that has been inherited.

Men and women today are faced with tremendous pressures from a fast-paced, seemingly unpredictable life. And men tend to have limited responses to stress, based on history. Most men have difficulty identifying tension and expressing emotions. Sometimes they may not even be aware they are stressed. Some women do the same thing. The difference lies in the fact that most women are more interpersonally and socially connected, making it a little easier to get support.

So, men in general, have to become more at ease with their stress, understand it's okay and normal to experience it. Men must really acknowledge that there's nothing wrong with them because they feel stress. In truth, avoiding this fact can be dangerous. Once the idea of having stress is normalized you can figure out what resources you have, and a solution is that much closer.

It's okay to get help! Many men still feel they're supposed to be able to solve everything themselves. As we said before, they equate asking for help with weakness. This belief often pops up when it comes to seeing a therapist. If you have to go to a therapist, you must be crazy. A man who is aware of himself, however, tends to see the ability to reach out as a strength. This man has the courage to solve the problem and actually feel better.

I am happy to report that the resistance seems to be loosening somewhat. More and more men are showing up in the therapist's office and that's a great sign of growth. I hear it in my daily life too, men talking and sharing with other men about personal concerns, not just football scores or cars. Of course, there isn't anything wrong with those topics. It's just about the freedom to expand your interests and express vulnerabilities as a part of strengths.

RESPONSE TO THREAT

The ways we navigate threat range from the instinctive fight or flight response, experienced first by our primitive ancestors, to the many complex responses felt both physically and emotionally in contemporary society. Any of these options serve as protective mechanisms in the face of danger. But in an attempt to protect itself, the whole physical body tenses and goes on alert. When we are drawn to fight, flight, or freezing (battle, run, or become paralyzed) the body attempts to manage and nullify the stress. Initially, the energy tends to be stored in the body until the threat passes. For the threat to be processed effectively this energy needs to be released. When successfully discharged, life progresses and moves on to the next experience. When the energy cannot be released, it becomes stored and eventually begins to accumulate with other experiences, and poses a long-term danger both physically and emotionally to the organism.

PHYSIOLOGY

Let's take a look at the physiology of what happens in the body in the face of a threat. When stress is experienced various hormones are secreted by the glands. The main hormone is cortisol, which is secreted by the adrenal glands, and readies the body and puts it on alert. It also triggers other glands in the body to secrete their own hormones for protection and further support. One of the many functions of cortisol is to turn off inflammation in the body. When too much cortisol is present in the body stress cells become desensitized to the hormone and inflammation increases. Inflammation damages blood vessels and brain cells over the long term and leads to insulin resistance, which is a precursor to diabetes. As a matter of fact, most doctors agree that stress is involved in some way with about 80 percent of all illness.

SCOPE

Stress ranges from chronic, deeply scarring trauma to milder, everyday pressure. Stressful experiences differ in intensity depending on the degree of the stimulus and the sensitivity and adaptability of the person. For example, everything else being equal, the intensity of being threatened at gunpoint would register far more trauma than being stressed by a barking dog. Again, some people could be more or less upset in response to the same stimulus based on their physical and mental constitution and history. Some are more adaptive to weathering stress and finding solutions to managing it. Confronting stress in its initial stages gives us the best advantage of tackling and effectively releasing the blocked energy because it hasn't yet become embedded or lodged in the system.

DEALING WITH STRESS

The ability to deal with stress effectively lies in how we perceive it and understand it. The Chinese character for danger and the character for opportunity are the same. It's both! You can choose to focus on one or the other. Perceiving the usefulness of an experience as opposed to the debilitating effects is an important factor in successfully processing that experience. This is especially true of stress.

Let's take the simple example of driving in traffic. This common activity usually brings about the best in us, right? You may be late for an appointment or preoccupied with something happening at the house. You may not have gotten enough sleep or maybe you just hate your job. Whatever it is, you're feeling so much tension that now you have become a madman at the wheel. You begin to take your anger out on everyone else on the road. It doesn't matter who or what at this point. It could be an old man driving sluggishly, or another frustrated driver like yourself speeding in and out of the lanes. What about that driver who all of a sudden decides to change lanes without signaling? Or the SUV bearing down on you when you are already feeling the world pressuring you? The tension begins to build in your body and the only outlet you see available to you is to scream and yell, or worse still, to start acting out those feelings by driving recklessly and aggressively. At the same time, you know these are not good ways to cope.

So, how to solve the problem? You can do this in two ways. You can either reduce the stressor or focus on positive coping mechanisms. Eliminating the stressor means removing what is causing the pressure. You might take an alternate route, for example, or leave earlier so you miss the traffic. The other approach, which in the case of traffic might be more useful, would be to develop positive coping mechanisms to deal with the stress. So, how do you that?

Let's consider three common ways we avoid dealing with the stress: 1. Distance from your feelings, not letting yourself know how much something is affecting you. 2. Blame others for the problem. 3. Substitute (triangulating) a third factor, which serves to deflect the real cause of the problem by creating a diversion. Do you recognize any of them?

You can deny the fact you are affected by stress. Yup, here you're out of touch with your feelings. Or, you can blame it on the other drivers and deny any responsibility for your own feelings. Most of us know this one well. Or, perhaps, you have a drink before getting behind the wheel, using alcohol to mediate the anxiety. Here we get to numb the feelings not only of the immediate traffic situation but possibly of the deeper, more hidden cause of the tension. Of course, it also adds another dangerous factor to the situation.

Okay, so let's get back to finding ways to deal *positively* with the stress. This approach will be helpful not only in the specific situation, but for the longer haul. What if you were to decide to give yourself a choice to change the way you're responding, and let yourself be open to treating yourself differently, instead of stressing yourself out and/or directing that frustration at others? Impossible in the moment? That's already embracing defeat, and setting up a framework that assures it will not happen. Belief is the important initial component in creating the result you want. If you don't believe that something can happen, it can't. Having a belief releases a directive energy toward the fulfillment of that belief. We talked about this earlier. Everything we see around us, from all of physical reality to the great works of the mind, was first conceived in the psyche of the person who created it. Belief motivated them to make concrete what was stimulating their imagination. If you believe it, you can conceive it!

First, we believe in possibility, and then we put it into action. Where you put your energy is where it will grow, negative or positive. Believing you can change yourself is the first step. Then knowing what you want the outcome to be completes the cycle. In this case, let's say you would like to be a calm, stress-free driver. The sought-after change (the outcome) should be both desirable and pleasing to you on some level. The pleasing result in this example will be the reduction of tension and the resulting feeling of calmness. The only thing left is to direct that energy toward your goal in the way that feels good.

You desire and believe you will reduce your stress. Then you change your emotional state. Decide to be that person who calmly responds to activated stress. This man refuses to let stress run him. He knows this can't be done by blaming or projecting blame onto others or expecting them to be different. He also knows that things like alcohol numb his system and don't allow him to focus on an effective solution.

The power to change lies within yourself, and that awareness can result in the action required to release the frustration and anxiety. It's amazing how with some practice you can begin to achieve a reduction of stress in various areas of your life. As you do this, you also may begin to understand the real cause of the stress and work to change it.

Let's look at a practical example of a man learning to deal with stress in a more constructive way both for himself and his son.

MEET JACK:

Jack is a single father of a fourteen-year-old son. Jack carried all the responsibilities of the single father. As with most single parents, he also worked a full-time job. Jack was fortunate that his mother was available and willing to care for her grandson and that there was an after-school program. The problem for Jack was in the morning, getting his son up and out for school and being on time for work. His son struggled to get up in the morning, and most mornings would not get out of bed. This led to a lot of arguments, which often escalated to physical confrontation. By the time Jack got to the office, he was not only late, but it took him awhile to simmer down so he could focus on his work. Two problems presented themselves. How could he get his son up on time? How could he accomplish this while reducing his own stress?

Jack came into my office one evening completely frustrated. He had attempted everything he knew to solve the problem. He felt defeated, but was open to new input and even more important was willing to stop trying to change his son and to look to change himself instead. He didn't know how, but saw this as an opportunity. His frustration was so high that it was hard to get any kind of perspective. The first thing he had to do was to gain control over his own emotional reactivity. This was not easy for him, especially since reacting impulsively had shown up in other areas of his life. "I've had this problem my whole life," he confessed. He said he always wanted to learn to control his feelings, but no one ever took the time to show him how. His father, typical of the men of his day, was emotionally distant from his son and overly involved in his own job. He also drank and tended to isolate himself. His mother cared for Jack, but had problems expressing her own feelings. He fended for himself as best as he could. Now, his family-of-origin patterns were playing themselves out in his current life.

We started by just getting him focused on what was happening inside. Being able to express himself and feel understood (by me initially) relieved a lot of the pressure. He soon saw very clearly that *he* had to change if his situation was to change. In assessing his strengths — intelligence and motivation among them — he believed he had the capacity to change. He also had external resources, including his mother and the school.

I further helped him access more of his inner strengths — honesty and commitment among them. To begin working on himself, we talked about how to control his feelings. He learned to close his eyes and start to observe himself in these situations with his son, and to begin to start practicing holding his emotional reactivity toward his son and visualizing his calm response. This took some practice. It was very difficult at first not to judge himself. He did not like what he saw. He was beating himself up for feeling and being so out of control. Still, he stuck with the practice and was becoming more confident. This gave him more motivation to change. But how could he modulate his emotional state?

I asked him where in his body he felt the stress? "In my stomach," he responded. I told him to imagine going into his stomach and observing what he saw. That was easy, "Lots of pressure!" In lieu of this pressure, did he want to reduce the stress? He said, "Let's go!" In a relaxed state, I instructed him to look around his stomach where he would find a meter with the numbers one through ten. This meter controlled the pressure: ten being the most intense. I had him play with the dial and eventually asked him what number his stress was at that moment. He answered, "Eight!" I asked him to slowly notch it up to nine. He felt the increase in pressure. Then I told him to dial it down to a six. He did, and he experienced some relief. Learning to play with this dial, he could check in with the stressful feelings to gauge their intensity, and then begin to exert some control over himself in those charged situations.

Jack not only used this tool to calm himself, he opened the door to more creative solutions in dealing with his son. For example, rather than the constant power-struggle with his son in the mornings, he decided to calmly tell him what time he needed him to be ready to leave, and that he expected him to be ready on time and that if he wasn't ready, he would be leaving without him. All this was said in a firm but caring way. Keeping it emotionally calm was important, because it allowed him to stay focused on his new goals — to get his son to school, be on time for work, and do it all with a minimum of stress.

The first day his son wasn't ready, and though Jack felt a little apprehensive, he left for work. He did communicate his plan with the school and the school was prepared to follow up with the next phase of the plan.

Young Jack walked downstairs in a state of fury and panic. He called his grandmother right away, screaming and yelling and accusing his father of busting his chops. Now, he would be in trouble at school! He asked his grandmother to take him to school, which she did willingly. Jack hadn't communicated the plan to his mother (ideally, he should have), and she thought her son was being a little bit extreme.

When he finally got to school, he not only received a late slip, he was told that any further problems in this area would get him detention. Jack, Jr., expressed a lot of anger when his father returned home that evening. Having spoken to his mother and the school during the day, Jack responded very calmly and coolly to his son. He was very clear that he would not be fighting or arguing with his son anymore about being ready on time in the morning. His son was complaining as he said this, and Jack even refused to engage him in that. He just repeated what he had said earlier. And, yes, his son was on time the next day and thereafter.

Jack got in touch with that part of his power as a man that allowed him to rise above the triggers. He took the opportunity and he had the courage to set limits and create structure for his son. He also used his softer side to engage his son and be kinder to himself.

What Jack Learned: Although he didn't think that his stress could be relieved, he learned some effective tools for lowering it. He connected that his stress could be alleviated by increased structure and lower levels of anxiety, and once he created that structure he saw how it could be an effective base for change. He also identified how his current situation related to his lack of structure as a child. He learned some relaxation exercises and other tools, such as inner imaging, which not only helped him to reduce tension but to make space for new behaviors. He realized that he could empower himself and take charge of his life.

———————

I am reminded of a story my brother told me many years ago about how he dealt with the stress of his kids driving him and his wife crazy by leaving their clothes and shoes around. No matter what he did to remind them, whether warnings or punishments, nothing was working. He warned them that if they didn't clean up, he would throw everything out. One day, determined to remedy the situation, he decided to gather up all the shoes and sneakers lying around, along with the shirts and jeans, and threw them in the garbage! The kids got up the next day and asked where they were. When my brother told them, they were furious and frantic. They raced outside and were able to recover their lost goods. It was an unusual remedy, but it did teach them to pick up their clothes. There was no more stress in this area.

BEFRIENDING STRESS

We've spoken about reducing stress when we are open and ready to deal with it, but what about when we can't express it, or when we're not even aware of it?

Stress is a natural part of life and everyone experiences it in one way or another. How you deal with it will determine whether it affects your life positively or negatively. Some people express stress outwardly, and others feel it, but don't express it. Some are afraid to release it. Still others are not aware of it. Men and women tend to have different ways of dealing with stress.

The body secretes cortisol and epinephrine when we have stress. To combat these hormones the brain secretes oxytocin, the so-called love hormone. One difference between men and women when it comes to stress is that more oxytocin is secreted in women. Most women will connect to a friend or family member and talk out their feelings. It is less common for men to verbalize their feelings of stress — to others and even to themselves. Men tend to default to the fight or flight response mentioned before. They either try to battle it or to ignore it in the hope that it will just go away. Truth is, many men tend to effectively reduce stress symptoms via physical activities such as working out, running, playing tennis, etc. This tends to burn off the immediate symptoms, but usually doesn't effectively address the cause. It's like having a leak in the hose. You can mop up the water on the floor, but the actual leak will remain unless you get to the source. Getting to the cause of the stress, and identifying the attached emotions, will help stop the cycle. The emotion and tension can be released and reframed so it doesn't keep cycling through the person's life.

A man must have the courage to be open to understanding the many ways that stress is manifesting in his life, in his relationships, and affecting his health and well-being. He must be willing to learn about how he may be holding it and how he may be taking it out on other people. He needs to see stress not as the enemy, but as a friend who can teach him its wisdom about how to make the most of his experience.

MEET ROBERT:

Robert, thirty-eight, is a very successful massage therapist with his own practice. He comes in close physical contact with people every day, but has spent most of his adult life struggling with intimacy in his relationships. After spending some time in an especially abusive relationship where he was emotionally abused, he made an appointment to see me. This was the pattern of his life, and he generally dealt with it by distancing himself with work and hobbies. Finally, he wanted to understand how he had developed this pattern. He began to see how he protected himself every time he was hurt, and that he had built up a negative image of women in general, seeing them as threatening and manipulative. He took responsibility for creating this pattern, or at least living inside of it, and realized that if he wanted to be different, he had to perceive it differently.

As he began to look critically at himself and his part in relationships, he started by allowing himself to feel some of his feelings, especially his fear of being hurt and his anger toward women. He recognized that he was permitting himself to be abused. Robert realized his feelings were okay to feel and that they represented a part of him that he was out of touch with. As he became more comfortable with his real feelings his confidence grew, his views expanded, and he began developing a more positive self-image.

What Robert Learned: He learned that he didn't have to run when he felt trapped or threatened, and that when he was in touch with his power, fear and stress could be reduced. He could see them as allies.

Victims of physical and mental abuse have been traumatized and they cannot process the experiences by themselves. They can benefit from professional assistance. Traumatic experiences are often held inside, embedding themselves in the body and in the psyche — both in the conscious and unconscious mind. Trauma holds on tenaciously as the victim of abuse shuts down against the threat of re-experiencing the pain with the emotional intensity of the original events. A competent trauma therapist can create a safe environment, and by reading the body signals can assist the individual in slowly releasing the stored experiences and reprocessing them, so they can be integrated positively back into the psyche. It's important for fathers and mothers to be aware of some of the possibilities of these treatments.

We need to make it safe for our children and teach them ways to process and express experience, no matter how difficult. Everyone encounters stress. How well we manage to process and express it is the difference between freedom and entanglement.

STRESS AT WORK

We've already pointed to stress created by the pace of our world as well as financial pressures caused by a fluctuating economy. These tend to be broad cultural pressures that affect the whole experience of work for most people. There are also pressures generated by specific jobs as well as the personal stress each person carries. Most people feel they are at the mercy of stress in their lives. In my experience, some stress you can't control and some you can transform by finding meaning. Finding meaning makes some experiences more positive. I have found that a lot of stress can be eliminated or at least greatly reduced when you're aware of it, take responsibility for changing it, and make solid steps to address it. Seeing stress as meaningful — assigning meaning when necessary — can serve to lessen its impact.

We can experience stress as positive, for example, when we meet a deadline or accomplish a goal. We can choose to use the pressure to move us toward the joy of reaching a target. The expenditure of energy spent in reaching a meaningful goal can actually be invigorating.

On the other hand, stress can be negative and infective. When we're stressed at work and don't know how to de-stress, we tend to bring it home with us. Many men and women wind up coming home and taking their frustrations out on a partner. And if they don't direct it towards their partner or children, they may continue to take it out on themselves. The solution for this is to be aware of what's frustrating us and look to direct it to the person or situation with whom or with which it belongs. Sometimes our partners can serve as a sounding board to help us decipher the stress. For example, one partner can help the other identify a problem at work when it may be expressing itself as a tension at home.

MEET DENNIS AND MELISSA:

Dennis, thirty-seven years old, and his wife Melissa, forty years old, are the parents of two young children: a five-year-old boy and a two-year-old girl. Dennis is a detective, a stressful job. Melissa works full-time from home and manages the kids during the day. They chose their busy schedule because they want to live a life they can afford. This situation generates a lot of stress. Dennis deals with his stress by going to the gym and working out. Melissa would like to work out, but feels she has no time. She complained to her husband that she needed his help and that he wasn't doing enough around the house. They weren't getting along. She became so overwhelmed by the stress she began having anxiety attacks which, of course, produced more tension for her.

Both wanted to reduce their stress. Melissa and I decided to meet for a couple of sessions and do some hypnosis and relaxation exercises. This approach worked and her anxiety attacks abated. She revealed as well that her father had deserted the family and had been in and out of her life. She also had a very distant and conflictual relationship with her step-father. She realized this "father problem" was playing itself out with her husband, and she wanted to solve the problem and make her marriage work.

Dennis had his own father problems. His parents were separated and his father was not there when he needed him. Fortunately, his maternal grandfather became a very warm and supportive father-figure for him. As the eldest child, Dennis was somewhat spoiled and entitled, usually getting his way. We worked on this issue, and he began taking more responsibility around the house.

What They Learned: This couple had the courage to face their stress and not run from it. They supported each other. Dennis was willing to express his feelings and seek help when he got stuck. Melissa was able to face her personal issues and her feelings of anger and disappointment. Both saw how the past might be influencing the current reality. They remain very present and effective parents to their two children.

Techniques for dealing with stress effectively:

1. Express rather than depress: Talk it out with someone, whether a friend, a partner, or a therapist. Moving the tension and pressure from inside the body to outside of it will not only relieve the pressure, it will provide an opportunity to understand it. When a feeling is processed, it often becomes clear and tangible and can be easier to change.

2. Write it out or draw it out: Take a piece of paper and write just like you feel it or draw an image of the feeling, no judgments. These methods tend to help flesh out and give some shape to the anxiety. You can see it right in front of you. You can also go back and feel into what you wrote or drew, perhaps getting

a better understanding as you can see it from different angles. Keeping a journal may also be helpful.

3. Exercise: Movement can be a great antidote to anxiety. You may not always arrive at an understanding of the origin of the stress, but you will usually get some relief from the effects. Regular exercise is also healthy for your whole body.

4. Using the breath: Deep, slow breaths bring in fresh oxygen to the body. When we're anxious, breathing is fast and shallow. We relax and reduce tension when we breathe slowly and deeply. Take a slow deep inhale to the count of 4, hold it for 7 seconds, and then release it slowly to the count of 8. Practice this for four cycles 2 times a day until you begin finding some relief. Use this breath approach to immediately calm the anxiety. It also helps with cravings and falling asleep, as well as slowing the heart rate and lowering blood pressure. Experts, such as Andrew Weil, MD, offer an array of breathing techniques. (www.drweil.com)

5. Tapping (Emotional Freedom Technique-EFT): This technique is a blend of Eastern philosophy and Western psychology. You physically tap on each of eight energy centers according to Chinese medicine using your fingertips at the same time as you allow yourself to feel and express your emotions about your stress. As you do this, you may become aware of feelings and/or bodily sensations arising in your consciousness. Staying focused on these while you tap allows the stress to be released. This process can be very positive, but the change tends to be gradual. Tapping has been shown to have excellent results overall with both positive short-term symptom relief as well as releasing some of the deeper causes of stress. And it's easy to do! (www.thetappingsolution.com)

6. Cognitive-behavioral techniques: In general, these techniques deal with the distortions in thinking that may cause us to hold onto stress, and encourage us to focus on the positive corrections we can make to help us resolve stress. Aaron Beck is the originator of this form of therapy. (www.beckinstitute.org)

7. Bi-lateral stimulation: This technique is from a helpful little book by Melissa Tiers entitled The Anti-Anxiety Toolkit: Rapid Techniques to Rewire the Brain (2011). It's a compilation of effective practices for stress relief. First, identify a part of the body that's holding stress and rate it from one to ten (with ten being the most intense). Then, holding a ball (or any object) out in front of you pass the ball back and forth from one hand to the other. As you do this, make sure the ball that's in your hand moving toward the midline crosses the midline of your body, as doing this fires up both hemispheres of the brain. This spreads blood and electrical impulses in the brain flooding the area of stress and lessening it.

8. The backward spin: This approach is also taken from the Tiers book as well. Locate the stress in your body and notice the direction of its flow and its speed (usually fast). Take your hands and mimic the movement. Imagine it moving inside your body. Then, move it outside your body, moving it in the same direction. Now, reverse the speed and the direction of the spin moving it back into your body. Notice how the stress feels different.

9. Dial it down: Finally, this imaging technique can also be found in the Tiers book, and I originally learned it as "Control Room" in a training some years back. I used it in the case example of Jack. When you feel stressed, visualize a meter with numbers from one to ten (with ten being the most intense). Note what number your stress registers and let yourself feel the stress. Now, turn the dial up one notch and feel the increase in pressure. Then, begin dialing it down. Experiment with the dial and notice how you can affect the levels of stress. (www.melissatiers.com)

10. Meditation: For a more long-term method of dealing with stress, meditation is a practice that reduces anxiety. Any form of mindfulness meditation or Transcendental Meditation™ can be helpful to explore.

11. Qigong or Tai Chi: The Eastern art forms of Qigong and Tai Chi are approaches that deal with balancing the body's energy (Chi) and relieving energy blockages created by stress.

12. Yoga: Similar to Tai Chi and Qigong, Yoga is a combination of breathing techniques, meditation, and physical body movements to achieve inner peace and happiness. It helps the mind and the body.

— 7 —

THE SPIRITUAL MAN

We come to an area of human development that is difficult to define but adds a very important element to who we are and what the quality of our lives can be. The term "spirituality" is a broad concept that encompasses a variety of different viewpoints. Most of these views have as a common thread the belief that in this universe there exists a power(s) greater than ourselves. This power is referred to as God, Allah, Great Spirit, nature, the universe, and by many other monikers. This power can be seen as transcendent, or intimately involved with our present life, and experienced as a sense of natural interconnectedness that fosters a feeling of peaceful engagement with the world. Some associate spirituality with a concrete institution such as a church, mosque, or temple. Others see it as a direct, personal relationship. This perception, like any belief, can change as our experience of life develops.

Some researchers and spiritual experts have their own definition of spirituality. A noted religious scholar, Christine Pulchalski, MD, Director of the GW Institute of Spirituality and Health, defines spirituality as: "The aspect of humanity that refers to the way individuals seek and express meaning and purpose, and the way they express their connectedness to self, to others, to nature and to the significant or sacred." Mario Beauregard and Denyse O'Leary, authors of *The Spiritual Brain*, see spirituality as any experience that brings the experiencer into contact with the divine (and not just any experience that feels meaningful).

Ruth Beckmann Murray and Judith Proctor Zenter define spirituality as a harmony with the universe, which is always striving to understand the infinite and "comes into focus when the person faces emotional stress, physical illness or death" (University of Minnesota, "Taking Charge of Your Health" series, "What is Spirituality?").

Are spirituality and religion the same thing? Most writers and researchers indicate that there is a difference between the two concepts but most agree that there is an area of overlap. Spirituality deals more with meaning in one's life, being connected with others, and how one relates to this great power. Religion pertains to more structural and ritualistic aspects of the various formal belief traditions. The two concepts are similar in a broad focus, including the necessity of belief, the importance of representing the meaning of existence, the experience of awe in the realization of the existence of non-physical reality, and comfort in times of adversity.

Some people grow up within certain religious beliefs and spiritual practices. During our lifetime as we experience its ups and downs, our beliefs may change, or we may lose some or all of the practices passed down by parents and gain new ones that reflect our own unique experience. Most people wish to live a meaningful life, but often we are not prepared when meaning takes on a different quality with new experience. It's important to evaluate new events and relationships as they can stretch our present beliefs making them more relevant to us. For example, most of us naturally change our perspective as we grow older, because at each stage of life we can see situations from a new viewpoint. We can choose to hold onto those beliefs that continue to satisfy us, and release those that don't serve us anymore.

I grew up in a very traditional religious family. We went to church every Sunday, said prayers before going to bed, and almost always said grace before meals. My parents were loyal to their religion and based most of the daily decisions on their religious principles. Most religions have their rules and practices, and I tried to follow our teachings as best as I could, because I believed God wanted me to be as perfect as I could be. I never felt perfect, and I had a lot of guilt. This is how I came to understand religion: Follow the rules and you'll be saved. This life isn't important. It is the next life that counts. I recognize that this is not the conclusion that everyone reaches.

I was just out of high school when I decided to go away to a religious community to study and become a teaching "brother". Everyone was shocked. Why was I doing this? I was taught by the brothers in the catholic school I attended and they seemed "cool". They played sports with us and you could open up to them easily. I wanted more of that. I felt that I couldn't miss! If I didn't like it, I could leave. Of course, I realized later the real reason I wanted to leave was to get out of my house and away from the limiting control of my parents and the belief system that gave their life the structure they wanted.

I didn't realize it but, I was moving into more structure! On two separate occasions, I wanted to leave but was talked into staying by members of the religious community. It would be a few years before I could make a decision for myself. When I finally did decide, it was the first time in my life, I made a major life decision of my own and even learned to take away some positives from my experience.

Religiously, I questioned everything. It was the beginning of a lot of confusion, but the start of a process of critical thinking and honesty that I carried for the rest of my life.

Despite the heaviness of the duty-bound philosophy in which I was raised, I came away with some basic learnings that I have carried with me always. The fundamental one was honesty. My father lived honestly himself, even to the point of being critical of his own errors in judgment (sometimes overly critical, I thought). I used to watch my father pray in church. He would close his eyes and I'd see his lips moving to the words he was praying. I felt his sincerity. Also, he and my grandfather, who was a trained operatic tenor, used to sing in the church choir. Their voices were dominant and would stand out from the rest of the choir. Sometimes I felt embarrassed as a child by the attention it would draw. But they were putting their all into it. They sang their hearts out, as a way of expressing their beliefs. They were true to themselves.

In addition to honesty, I learned about loyalty to one's family and church and it sewed a very important seam in my life that played itself out later on in my relationships with family and friends. It became a very important element in making any kind of commitment.

For example, the obvious value of loyalty for me rested in the allegiance I could bring to my relationships and the dedication I could bring to my work. On the downside, loyalty sometimes led me to hang onto things too long, like relationships that drained me of energy and emotion because I had to stick by them no matter what.

My early religious education offered limited views of what a spiritual path could be for me, but because I lived in a broader world and was a product of the 1960s, I later had the opportunity to think differently. I chose to grapple with the outcomes of my own life experiences as they rubbed up against what I believed. It has resulted in a belief system that is alive because it is mine, and it has given me a meaningful focus on the quality of how I want to live.

TESTING BELIEF

As we go through the various ups and downs of life, experiencing its many intricate threads, we can deepen and learn more about ourselves and what our interests and strengths might be. Using these elements purposefully can bring us much satisfaction as well as allow us to contribute to the richness of our close relationships and to society in general.

The spiritual path is not always easy, as some of life's events can be incomprehensible to us, seeming to defy the assumptions and expectations of our spiritual belief system. Certain events can create a crisis of faith and bring about periods of depression, anger, or doubt. Some of us are sent into a tailspin and find we have to reevaluate the meaning of our beliefs. Some of us are going through this level of questioning right now brought on by COVID and the social unrest that is throwing us off kilter.

MEET ANTHONY:

Anthony is a sixty-three-year-old married man with two adult daughters living on their own. I asked him about whether he had a spiritual belief system and how it developed. Growing up, he had lived in a traditional religious home, going to church on some Sundays and holidays and praying on a regular basis. He attended the men's weekend gathering in his church basically at the behest of his wife, who encouraged him to go, and because he had seen the positive effects a woman's group had had for her. On the weekend, he had gotten a lot out of sharing his feelings and hearing others share theirs. So, he committed to monthly group meetings and he continued to develop his faith and allow his present belief system to grow.

At a certain point, however, encounters with heartache challenged all that he had found. One of his daughters developed a drug problem and became so depressed that she wanted to die. The experience brought him to his knees, causing him to question whether there was a God. He was very depressed and angry. Eventually, though, his daughter was able to get back on track. She became a very capable counselor, a testament to her own ability to take life's adversities and create something good from them.

Anthony was also able to regain a connection with his own beliefs because of the positive changes in his daughter. He also credited his wife's strength and faith as having carried them both through. Anthony confesses he may not have been able to return to his faith if things with his daughter hadn't changed. We will never know.

Of course, we are all different. Under the same conditions, some people might have actually become stronger in their beliefs whether or not she had improved. Others might have dropped their faith when she first got into trouble. Still others might have turned to evaluate and change their beliefs in the face of her challenges. Is one's spirituality based on the expectation that we can through our prayers to a higher power or in some other way control the outcome of certain events?

What Anthony Learned: He realized that faith has many dimensions. Faith is more than just a way to control events and have them change in the way we expect. Faith can be an enduring belief in our truth of an experience no matter what the result. He admitted his questioning around this as part of his truth. His faith proved valuable to him as his daughter recovered. He acknowledged and accepted the strength and support of his wife.

———————

As we navigate the vicissitudes of life, we "let go" and "take in" and we attempt to retain all that's valuable and essential to us. As in all relationships, the relationship to spirituality asks vulnerability, commitment, and a living into belief. Faith is an ongoing lived experience that we continue to evaluate as we grow.

We try to leave behind old beliefs and practices that don't serve us anymore, as we integrate and learn new ones. Changing or adapting present beliefs and opening to new ones takes a certain vulnerability and strength of character. This is part of our humanness—to be able to adapt and to change.

Some people believe we have an essence, or a soul that is whole and uniquely us. This belief holds that this essence is the true core of who we are and is connected with the divinity in each of us and all living things. A snake sheds the old skin so it can develop a new one, but its essence remains. A caterpillar outgrows its cocoon, as it fulfills its purpose in becoming a butterfly, and more fully itself, but its essence remains!

SURRENDER AND FAITH

There are many aspects of life that we can't control. Even though we work hard to be consistent and effective in mapping our lives, it doesn't always turn out the way we planned. Things happen that defy our comprehension. With those things that we can't control, we look to develop an explanation that gives us meaning about why. This involves a letting go of the need to be sure based on our explanation for why things happen.

An important concept of many spiritual belief systems is surrender. Surrender means yielding our wills and our efforts to control the outcome of events in our lives, whether to God, to the natural process of the universe, or to the power that is greater than us.

Many of us fight life in an attempt to get the results that we want, even though we have no actual control over what does and doesn't happen. Such futile efforts can cause tension and anxiety. By surrendering and reframing painful or incomprehensible events in the light of new meaning, we allow ourselves to integrate the lessons and calm the tendency toward internal friction and, more important, we make meaning.

The whole idea of surrendering can have a negative connotation in the competitive world of men. We are taught that to surrender is to lose, to be weak. But we are, as a species, beginning to learn that surrender has a larger meaning, one not confined to sports events or war. It can signify an opening of the self to the other so that authentic giving and receiving is possible. All good relationships are built on exchange, on give-and-take. The evolved man knows surrender as strength and can see this as an avenue to greater involvement in life. Surrender is essential to faith.

Faith is a response to not knowing and to what we don't get to control. Surrender is taking a leap of faith and trusting our own sense of what we believe to be true.

MEET BEVERLY:

Beverly is a lifelong spiritual seeker. Growing up with a religious mother, Beverly rebelled against anything religious and was a non-believer in the early part of her life.

However, she continued to search for meaning and right before a very serious eye operation, she had an experience of the "felt sense of a spirit" supporting the upper portion of her body. It felt wonderful, and she suddenly understood that she had not been allowing herself to receive and feel supported. She thought of herself as someone who was "responsible to figure everything out herself, and didn't need any support." This was creating a lot of undue anxiety for her, and she realized she was trying to control the outcome of many events in her life. She stated, "I needed to surrender some of the controls, but I had so much anxiety I had to face in doing so." How would she learn to release some of that effort?

When her husband died, she faced the question on an even deeper level. She experienced his death as a devastating loss and she had a very hard time dealing with it. She was angry at the God she believed took him from her. When she shared her grief and anger with the rabbi, he said: "It's all God, everything that happens." Over time, she thought about his words and began to comprehend that God may not be a person who's controlling life, but a force intimately involved with all of life (and death) and growing with her. She surrendered the belief that she needed to control events, or control the God who did, and opened to a new perspective: "You either trust life or you don't."

What Beverly Learned: In realizing she ultimately had no control over life, she was able to let go of the futility of that effort. Speaking with the rabbi allowed her to see things in a new way, to trust and to release the anxiety bound up in the need to control. She connected some current habits with past issues of needing to figure everything out herself and not letting herself depend on anyone else for support.

RITUALS AND SPIRITUAL PRACTICE

Rituals are ceremonies or routines practiced that reflect particular beliefs, often in a religious community. Religious rituals can be very meaningful in giving us support and aligning us with a sense of purpose. We may also take on certain spiritual practices that give life significance. Regular practice can ensure a continuous flow of meaning, and the more something is practiced, the more anchored in our psyche it becomes.

But habit can work the other way too and create a state devoid of meaning. It can become ritualized and rote, doing for the sake of doing. If this happens, a lot of the emotion and power can be drained from us. Most people who care about the effectiveness of their spiritual practices look for ways to renew the sense of significance through their practices. Perhaps a practice has become stale and can be refreshed, or maybe the fact that one idea of meaning has lost its appeal and will lead to a new, more expansive sense of meaning.

MEET BECKY AND BEN:

Both in their late fifties, Becky and Ben are the parents of three very successful young adult children, the youngest of whom is still in college and performing well above average. Spiritually, Ben grew up in a very orthodox religious community where ritual was sacred and meaningful. Becky, on the other hand, was raised culturally Jewish but with no spiritual framework. She decided the children would be raised with the religious structure that her husband experienced. She explained: "I wanted them to have what I didn't have — a good, solid religious base and a sense of community."

The family was steeped in religious ritual that gave their life a sense of peace. Becky enjoyed the religious ritual, finding a lot of comfort in the bonding experience it created for her family. At the same time, she had what she described as a "very scientific mind" and couldn't believe in anything that could not be verified. For example, she had an overwhelming fear of death, which she understood to have come as a result of her mother's death when Becky was two years old. Organized religion wasn't able to bring her any peace with regard to this, even when it spoke about an afterlife.

One day a friend introduced her to a spiritualist, who shared some insights about Becky and her family. This was what she deemed an "extraordinary experience," and she wondered how this person could know about her life in such detail. She also described this as a felt experience, and not solely an intellectual one, which she said added to belief.

Becky became interested in her spirituality, as she explored other non-physical experiences. She expressed that these spiritual experiences changed her whole life. She began to believe that all people may have an inner energy that they may not understand, and that may not be extinguished at death. As a result of this shift in her beliefs, she began to see the quality of her life improve. She felt freer and less encumbered with life's uncertainties, and she reported having no more fear of death.

What Becky and Ben Learned: They adopted certain religious rituals as a way to positively anchor the family in their belief system. Becky respected her own skepticism while also remaining open. She acknowledged and followed what she deemed a spiritual awakening. Becky and Ben found meaning in spirituality in their own ways, and used this layer of experience to improve the quality and meaning of their lives.

Over the centuries, religion has been a very unifying experience, positively satisfying the spiritual needs of many people. It has also served as the basis of most wars and resulted in much bloodshed. Under the guise of positive intentions, much destruction has occurred in the name of religion. The persecution of Jews, of Catholics, of Hindus, of Moslems, of Atheists throughout the world, historically and in the present, pit people against each other. Religion and politics have always been strange bedfellows, where prejudice is disguised in myriad ways. This is part of the very human aspect of spirituality, where anger and aggression are used to justify destructive acts towards others.

For my part, I believe the Universe has a "mind" of its own, and why things happen may never be fully understood. The spiritual man and woman surrenders to this unknowing, and honestly acknowledges what can be changed and what can't, and in so doing finds the courage and gratitude to act in accord with their spiritual beliefs. With humility and strength, they can find the courage to make the changes that they can make in their own lives. They can learn from the unexpected or intended events and integrate them as acceptable parts of themselves. And, they can find support systems that can help them to do that.

The spiritual man is at a crossroads. He must learn to respect other belief systems and look to learn from them and to work cooperatively with those views rather than seek to erase them. Recognizing the systems that are destructive and oppressive, the evolved adult may look to challenge them and speak out for the rights of those who suffer under them.

At their best, religion and spirituality can provide meaning and hope for humankind. This level of belief helps us as we navigate the unexplainable aspects of existence. The spiritual man can use this dimension to maximize the quality of his own life and support others in finding their own meaning.

— 8 —

THE EVOLUTIONARY MAN

WHO WE CAN BE: QUALITIES OF
THE AWAKENED ADULT

Some of us have an unclear and limited picture of who we are — and are uncertain about our possibilities and potential. Others are stretching their imagination and taking some risks to move out of self-limiting beliefs in an effort to see more options. These men realize that they are not solely defined by their past, and can work in the present to be more of what they envision.

This period of history calls for a man who has a broader focus and is able to address the needs of a culture looking for a positive direction: looking to men to come from the heart, with everything, including sensitivities, courage, and generative/procreative skills. The world needs more than sperm donors. We need men who are willing to become involved in a transitional culture no matter the growing pains. We need men to help themselves as well as helping others find their place in society. We need men who can teach positive values in an inclusive way.

The evolved man knows himself and is connected to who he really is. He can be vulnerable to others and can express his emotions. He can empathize with people and their life circumstances and tries to do his best to help them. He makes mistakes and is not afraid to own up to them. He understands that many men are depressed, ensnared in their personal choice to remain unaware or unwilling to face the possibility of change. Upholding the repressive ways of patriarchy reflects a fear-driven perspective and leads to destructiveness. The awakened man wants to encourage others to expand from their personal cocoons, to be open to new ways of thinking, and to express their needs and opinions in ways that celebrate their own voices without erasing others. This man teaches by example. If he gets stuck, he's not afraid to ask for help. He really understands that it's not a weakness to seek help — in fact, it reflects confidence and strength.

The evolutionary man also looks to understand his partner. He realizes her strengths and weaknesses and seeks to work with her as a valued co-partner. Wanting her to be her best self, he encourages her to do what she needs to do to be that, even if it may be at odds with his own thinking. Allowing other paths to unfold can be very challenging for some men, but hanging in there and working out a compromise can teach us a lot about ourselves and even strengthen our relationships.

In order to grow, men need to continue moving inward to expand their nonphysical selves. Developing the dimension of spirituality or qualities of character is an area that can help propel a man to expand. Such internal growth can help him realize his real power.

Let's take the concept of strength. A man's strength is generally associated with his physical prowess, especially in the area of sports and competition where the strongest and toughest and fastest are victorious. This association between strength and physical power applies to many other areas of life. An example might be in the work place, where strength and toughness have traditionally defined what makes a successful leader. Even in politics, politicians who are the loudest and most aggressive are often perceived as the most powerful. Might makes right.

In his book, Power vs. Force (2014), David R. Hawkins, MD, PhD, distinguishes between the two concepts. Force is energy that is connected to the emotions and fueled by the senses and is basically physical in nature, whereas, power is realized through an inner awareness and the expanding consciousness of our potential selves. It is basically non-physical and non-invasive by nature and effortless in expression. This unseen world (the universe) holds this powerful potential for us.

If we return to our example of strength and place it in this context, strength can be seen not only as a physical force, but as a certain quality of character — the courage to overcome fear, the capacity to feel painful emotions, or the bandwidth to access compassion when the impulse is to be hateful.

The modern adult can be empowered by perceiving qualities in a broader, fuller way. Strength can be seen as an inner quality. The reframe is radical and paradigm-shifting: Asking for help is not a weakness and helping others to be themselves is not a betrayal of competition. We can begin to see these dimensions as inner strengths. These are ideas on the cusp of transformation.

BECOMING LEADERS IN OUR OWN LIFE

We need men who can take a leadership role in their workplace and in their personal lives. It may start with finding work that is meaningful and that contributes to a growing need in society for a more positive direction.

Men in positions of leadership — as fathers, in education, in the helping professions, in the corporate world, in the spheres of law and enforcement — need to focus their specific attention on ethical ideas and fair behavior. Integrity is primary among the evolved man's characteristics.

As evolved adults, men and women can work equally in any job that suits their talents and interests. The field of technology will continue to evolve, and the structure of the workplace will assuredly continue to change. Cathy Benko, author of *The Corporate Lattice* (2010), explains that companies that once functioned according to the hierarchical model (decision-making from top down) are now encouraging more freedom of expression with the power and movement of decision-making moving more laterally. This structure allows for creative ideas to emerge, and keeps pace with a society that is increasingly entrepreneurial. It allows people at the grassroots level to have as much of an opportunity to input into the creative process as the upper level executives. Philippe DeRidder, founder of the Board of Innovation, says: "There are plenty of real life examples that show people are more motivated if they themselves make the decision rather than have a decision forced upon them." The freedom of this model encourages the work force to be more creative and more involved. This paradigm shift will necessitate new ways of thinking and operating. It may be the ability to fit into new work structures like this that will help to ensure successful employment for the future adult. And, as financial protectionist Unum suggests in a report called "The Future Workplace" (2015, The Guardian.com), businesses may need to work more collaboratively as they advocate to maximize the creation of new ideas.

The previous model of a single wage earner holding one job supporting a family is close to disappeared. My father had one job his whole life. I've already had three jobs, and usually a part-time job concurrently. Our children are working in an even more fluid world, moving more quickly from one position to another, sometimes holding multiple jobs simultaneously and often working remotely, especially now. There may be increasing opportunities to choose work that's both productive and satisfies our interests and abilities.

We also will need to be leaders in our personal and family lives. As men and women, we need to be in charge of the pace of our lives and that of our children, so we can set an example of healthy family functioning. We have to learn to adjust to an accelerating technology that even challenges the skills of young people and often promotes a level of isolation. We need to keep up without giving up … compassionate interaction, respectful encounter, courageous care.

We can step out to take active leadership positions on social issues such as prejudice and abuse, addiction, poverty, and the isolation of our elders. It's good for the world and for our own well-being. We are faced with new challenges every single day. Awakened adults stand up for their values, and teach their children respect and the importance of equity across race, gender, ability, and belief.

SETTING LIMITS

We often look upon children in contemporary society as entitled, what we once might have referred to as spoiled. This may be so in some cases, but in truth something else is likely going on: Shifting family structures wherein the parents do not take the lead and children are "parentified" by default, if not by design, makes it unsafe to be kids. For children to feel safe enough to leave control to others, they must feel that someone is in control. When the position of parent is lost in the shifting sands of change, a child may step in — become pushy, demanding, or a know-it-all. They are being put in a situation where they assume positions of power that they are not yet mentally and emotionally equipped to handle.

In this world where many children are left adrift, are unmotivated to learn and at the same time dealing with a shifting family power structure, it becomes even more important for parents to take charge and create new, workable structures where individuals can feel safe, productive, and happy. They can become mentors to their children and/ or help them identify others from whom to learn.

Fathers need to be willing to set limits and create structure for their kids, to foster, inspire, and model self-discipline. These are lessons that last a lifetime. Our children benefit when parents strive to be honest with themselves as well as others. We need fathers who are willing to be involved in their children's lives, to be there for their kids when they are looking for wisdom and guidance. There was a time when this was not easy — when men went out to work, often had very long hours and sometimes traveled far from home, and everything fell to women.

The world is different now. This is the time to make time for fathers to deepen and update the meaning of fatherhood.

MEET MONIKA:

Monika is a single twenty-four-year-old woman whose father was not around when she was growing up. "In the emotional and communicative sense...he shut himself off from my family," she explained. All she wanted was his approval, and she would vie with her sister for his attention. Growing up she didn't always behave, as there was a lot of disorganization in the house. Her parents didn't get along and there always seemed to be fighting. "My sister and I ruled the roost! There were no consequences or repercussions when we behaved poorly! We did whatever we wanted. Somebody would always fix it if it was broken."

Fortunately, Monika later found a male mentor in one of her bosses. She described, "He was patient and generous and taught me about life." He gave her financial advice and worldly wisdom, telling her to never take things too seriously and to look out for people who look out for you. She needed a safe structure and a patient ear.

The truth is that Monika was lucky because this need for structure and mirroring in a young person can sometimes lead down some unpleasant alleys in search of the "missing father" in someone who is not safe to confide in or lean on. The evolved man is a great father, not by virtue of his perfection, but by his comfort with imperfection and commitment to presence.

Many men haven't been as connected as they would like to be and would like to become more involved, but do not know what to do. How do we learn the lessons we didn't receive? As stated earlier, looking for mentors or reaching out for a counselor or a trusted friend, joining a men's group, reading self-development books — all are practical options that men can use to explore ways to become more involved.

Change can come from many places. It can begin with a feeling of unhappiness or an awareness of a deeply felt need. Being in touch with these feelings can ignite the fire of change. Sometimes change comes about in the wake of a transition, such as death of a parent, divorce, or job loss, which can result in a new level of perception and/or new behavior.

As a man becomes more successful in applying the new behavior and enjoys the result, he is encouraged by his own experience to make more changes. This is a familiar path for many men who are already committed to change.

We've all had those "aha!" moments when all of a sudden we understand something in a new way. It comes in a flash of realization. Sometimes we don't take the opportunity to do something with them, but we can. The "aha" can be integrated into a new way of being.

MEET ELLIOTT:

Elliott is forty-seven-year-old father, who grew up without a father in his life. What made him want to commit to being a better man? Elliott explained: "Positive role models are a must, but more important a person has to have the desire to be a better man and father. All of the education, training, community outreach/mentoring programs and professional services in the world mean nothing to a person who is not willing to receive the information and incorporate it into their lives!" What did being a better man mean to him, and what influenced him to change and be different from his own father? He explained, "I didn't want to be like my father. What I wanted was a strong role model and guiding force in some of my early decision making, but he wasn't around!" Elliott swore he would work hard and have a profession that meant something to him, and he would be there for his kids. This is what motivated him.

He worked to be that role-model he missed growing up both in his life as a dad and as a police officer.

The awakened man must be present to his relationships — willing to facilitate good decision-making whether in his private life or the workplace. Ideally, he's a man who can structure and balance his own life so that he has the time to give his best to each area of his life as he sees fit. A real leader works to do better with his own struggles before he attempts to lead others. Developing compassion for oneself helps us to realize what others are going through. There's a story about Mahatma Gandhi in *The Way of the Peaceful Warrior* (Millman, 2000): A mother brought her young son to Gandhi and asked Gandhi to tell her son not to eat sugar. Gandhi paused, and then told the woman to bring him back in two weeks. Feeling a bit confused, the woman obeyed his wishes and brought him back two weeks later. Pausing again, Gandhi looked the boy straight in the eye and said: "Stop eating sugar!" The woman was very grateful but asked him why he couldn't have told him the same thing two weeks prior. Gandhi replied: "Two weeks ago, I was eating sugar."

Different experiences serve as motivation for men to make changes. It may be the birth of a child, the death of a parent, or the loss of a job that is the catalyst for change. For some, these are moments of opportunity in addition to their other meanings. The evolved man tries to find meaning for himself in as many experiences as he can.

LIFE HAPPENS

Arthur, who is thirty-six years old, spent most of his twenties battling the law, without any purpose to his life. When he began reading self-help books, he started thinking about things differently, but he continued bouncing around with little direction. At a certain point, he met a woman and they decided to have a child together. The birth of this child marked Arthur's rebirth: "It's just something that happened! It was not until she was born that she became everything to me. I felt a great motivation to care for her."

Sal, whom we met earlier, explained : "I became a man after I graduated from college and went out on my own from a financial perspective...I became more of a man when I married my wife and we started our own life."

A talented massage therapist, Robert, whom we also met previously, came into therapy two weeks after breaking up with his girlfriend. He had been depressed and anxious. He reported, "I'm not good with relationships, and I don't trust women." But then he added, "I'm confused and messed up. It is time to get serious about my life." This marked his turning point: He had become so isolated and depressed, he admitted he couldn't deal with his life anymore and he finally sought help.

Jason and Eva (thirty-nine and forty-one) had two young children ages four and two. They were conflicted about how much work each of them contributed to the couple relationship. Jason claimed he was doing everything, and Eva, who worked nights, said she was doing the best she could with her time. Both cared for the children and respected each other as parents, but they were not always happy with each other. I saw them for four sessions over a four-month period. Their schedules were too busy to make a more consistent commitment. Truthfully, they were not ready to make the changes they thought they wanted to make. They took the first step though, and maybe it will pave the way for other opportunities to address their issues. Change is a commitment for which we must be ready.

DEVELOPING THE SKILLS THAT REAL CHANGE REQUIRES

Besides the desire to change, you must possess the tools to make that change. Everyone has the ability, but the internal resources have to be located first. If you're not able to realize them yourself, finding someone who can help you do it is a good step. You want to activate those assets, and then practice, practice, practice. Making the choice to attend your daughter's soccer game, making time to have a catch with your son, taking the responsibility for making that alimony payment on time, doing volunteer work, making a counseling appointment—these are all illustrations of claiming one's position, and they reflect commitments of presence to oneself.

After you act on the change, even a little, you can notice what it feels like to shift out of an old pattern. Really let yourself experience the decision. There may be an immediate sense of relief. Or, it may be disorienting for a second, and then comes relief! And when you take the first steps in the process, it will feel great, tapping into something you didn't even know you had! Even small steps can move us out of our stuck-ness. Many men begin to sense a new richness and a sense of freedom in what they receive when they begin to transform old patterns into new plans.

Even so, it's still difficult for most of us to cut loose from well-worn attitudes, even if they confine us. Most people find it hard to break out of the little boxes that they inhabit. Being trapped and feeling protected often go hand-in-hand. It's the devil we know.

Still, people do change, regardless of the circumstances of their upbringing. Even within the same family, one sibling will be motivated to expand options whereas another won't. This tells us something about freedom. It gives us hope that regardless of the family script, we can decide to be the sibling who can.

Mentors can play an important role in our action plan. One way to stoke our motivation is to find someone who has made the changes that we seek for ourselves and whom we admire.

MEET ISAAC:

Isaac is a thirty-year-old man whose father abandoned the family when Isaac was a baby. Isaac was able to create his own image of what a father could be under the positive influence of his step-father, as well as the various role models he adopted along the way. Some of his role-models were from real life and others were characters from the media. He explained, "I always seemed to gravitate to men who could overcome obstacles in their lives. The most important thing I learned about being a man is to keep my word. In my world, the only thing I have is my word. At times, I find that I have a problem disconnecting from my feelings in my relationships. Maybe it's because of my background and my father leaving the family. It's not always good, but I'm working on it!" Isaac wants to be a man of his word who can be depended upon, and a father who is present for his child.

Most men I've interviewed have been influenced by the lives of other men. Often, this influence enhances their picture of what a man can be. It happens whether they have a father who is active in their lives or not. As we develop as individuals, we may find that our present role models are limited in what they can teach us as we keep going down our path. Through the course of our lives, we encounter men and women to whom we are drawn because they offer something positive to us and inspire us to model their behavior. Of course, sometimes we may be mimicking something less than positive and it is important to understand the nature of what draws us. You ask yourself, is it a life-affirming role-model or a replication of something old, something negative?

There are a lot of dangerous alleys. Consider, for example, a young man who's looking to empower himself as a man and find a place to belong. He may become enamored with a local gang leader, who can fuel his random energy and give it direction. It fills his immediate need for belonging, but will almost surely be counterproductive in the end.

PASSING THE TORCH

We all carry our parents inside of us, they are in our DNA. I didn't realize the extent to which my own parents had influenced me until I was in my mid-twenties. Growing up in the 1960s and 1970s I experienced them as traditional parents, what I knew. The roles in my house were familiarly defined with some exceptions. One exception was that Dad cooked and all four children learned to cook. He even taught my mother how to cook.

Growing up, my mother was my biggest challenge, as well as one of my finest teachers. She had strong judgments about people and both parents held narrow opinions, especially about people outside their belief system. My mother taught me about emotions though, and was a very intuitive person. She understood some of the deeper motivations that drive people.

The most important things I learned from my father were in who he was as a person and the values he lived. Honesty and reliability were central to his being. He held me accountable anytime I tried to stretch the truth, and to this day, I tend to feel a tinge of guilt whenever I am not completely honest with myself or in relationship. Duty and responsibility were at the forefront for him and you couldn't find a more loyal person (even to the point of blind loyalty). He had a belief system and he lived it. Because honesty was so important though, he had to admit to himself and others when he made mistakes, and at those rare times when life events may have fallen short of his belief system.

Women can be mentors for men:

Many women are mentors for men. It's the qualities of a person, regardless of gender, that have the greatest impact on others. One client described his mother as his hero, the anchor in his life.

As another example, Emma's father was only around in the very early years of her life. Initially, like many children, she blamed herself. When she was young she also blamed her mother for his absence. Gradually, as she grew up, she understood that her father had many problems that had nothing to do with her.

Emma also had an older half-sister who cared for her when her mother was not home. Like most siblings they could get on each other's nerves, but as Emma matured she began to understand the impact her mother and half-sister had on her. She explained, "I learned to feel good about myself from my mother and my sister. They were my mentors."

Many years ago, I worked in a foster care agency, and as a budding administrator and clinical supervisor, I was looking to grow and learn. Marjorie, the director to whom I reported, helped me to gain the confidence I needed, and helped me to think through the many critical situations I had to face. We also learned to work cooperatively with the other departments. She was truly a mentor to me.

Being a mentor is a great responsibility. Anyone who has mastered a process, or embodies a desired skill, can be a mentor. Many supervisors find themselves in a position to teach and to transmit to others essential knowledge and effective ways of working together. There can be great joy and a deep level of satisfaction in mentoring. Knowing that you have made a difference in the life of another person can be satisfying and knowing that the person may pay it forward becomes a rich legacy.

THE IMPORTANCE OF CONNECTION

As a man awakens to himself, he can begin to notice and feel the complexities of his life and the many options that lie before him. He experiences himself in a much fuller sense, and the possibilities that are open to him. He may feel more connected to the world, or be aware of more nuances in his relationships. This is an outcome of expanded consciousness, moving from limited perception to an expanded understanding of the interconnectedness of life. This experience of relatedness to things around him can be supportive and generate a sense of belonging. This sense can make all the difference as he moves from hesitant participation in life to more active involvement. Most men feel excited when they realize the power of being connected, and they want to experience more of it.

Many men know how to connect. They know the importance of connections in the business world, in their social relationships, and in raising their children. They know the importance of investing the time it takes to close a business deal, or devoting the time to enjoy a sporting event with other men. There's always an opportunity to take what you know how to do in one area of your life and translating those skills into another.

Finding what interests you in the sphere in which you would like a better connection, and then applying the skills to develop that interest, can be a good way to start. Relationships can suffer when you hold back your gifts because you don't identify what brings meaning. The contemporary man can work to find quality time for close relationships and the activities that positively contribute to their evolving role as men.

BECOMING THE CHANGE WE SEEK

So, if we know of other men who may be interested in changing their lives, how can we support each other in making those changes?

One great way to gain the support that is so essential to shifting a life is to join a men's group. I have mentioned being a part of one myself. Your local community center or social service agency probably has information. But you know what? If you can't find one, start one. Network with other men who are working on improving their skills and quality of life. A group begins with two — and one of them is you!

My personal growth path has been shaped in part by my participation in a men's group for the past nineteen years. The opportunity to come together and share our feelings and perspectives has enriched our identities as men, including as fathers. It has given us a forum to ask questions, open up about our frustrations, and to celebrate what we have discovered.

A men's group serves as a place to take some deep breaths, and shed the tensions of the day, and so much more. It's a place to learn to share with other men who may have similar feelings and experiences or to benefit from different viewpoints — and to offer yours. You can explore new areas of possibility for yourself and try out new behaviors in an atmosphere of openness and trust. Bonds develop — not because they have to but because they can.

I have found that an important part of the success of the group involves the structure and the philosophy of how the group is run. It is important that privacy and confidentially are respected. Although it is not a therapy group, confidentiality is key to establishing a sense of safety and respect. In line with this sense of safety is a basic rule that has sustained the group: there is no place for criticism or advice-giving.

A man who is willing to open up around his feelings experiences release. Such release is not only for him but for those bearing witness. It offers a way for him to explore his inner world and be in good company as he does it. Others may ask questions, or choose to relate their own experiences, but there's no finger-pointing or armchair analysis. The question of working with a professional outside of the group sometimes may come up as a possibility for further exploration if desired. This is not within the purview of the group, however!

In the process of exchange, some men wind up confronting themselves and their old beliefs. Many of our own values are so firmly rooted, we have never thought to question them—and they can be difficult to change even if we decide it's a good idea. We often encounter our own parents inside of us—the ways their belief systems have influenced us when we weren't looking just as they were influenced by their parents.

If we're honest with ourselves, we can emerge from this process knowing who we really want to be and not just how we've been defined by others.

The awakened man is committed to building a social order that injects new meaning and creates positive structures to protect that meaning, as we continue to navigate the frenetic world of today. This man also looks to bring a humanizing quality so that people can be less isolated and their connections can feel enriched. He focuses on strengths, his own and on those with whom he comes into contact.

The evolved man can contribute his share by waking up from his long slumber and finding a place to weigh in — on global issues and local trends — with an involvement that means something positive to the culture and to the children, his and everyone's.

EPILOGUE

THE WAY FORWARD

Throughout the book, we've spoken about the importance of men emerging more fully developed both emotionally and psychologically. Western culture sorely needs competent, effective fathers who are present to their children and can teach them about their emotional selves and about a man's soft side. And it needs generous mentors who can help guide those who missed out on consistent positive role models. Once they understand this about themselves — that men have psychological needs for closeness and connection — they can teach it to others.

Society can benefit from positive and productive business and political leaders, individuals who can be respected for being honest, ethical, and compassionate. Such men will have an increased social and ethical awareness to contribute more effectively to a society in great need of healthy order and positive leadership.

In a world of increasing divisiveness and uncertainty, our children need men and women who through their actions and vision provide a model that teaches and encourages them to live with tolerance and love. Allowing them to step confidently and kindly into their own futures will be the great gift in a transforming world. The internal compass in times of transformation is an essential tool. That compass must be revealed, encouraged, supported.

Haven't we met people on our journey through the pages of this book who found ways to make important changes in their lives? These changes came when they were ready, willing, and able to take the step. And each one made a change in their own special way, by challenging their old beliefs and stubborn patterns from the past. This is the central process of building the qualities that define the awakened man and woman.

It starts with examining one's own beliefs and being willing to challenge stale patriarchal constructs of men and how they function. These old limiting beliefs endowed men with the power to control the evolution of society, but limited their opportunities to develop in other areas, including developing emotional intelligence and the language that conveys it. All of these elements are key in the development of intimacy. Transformation for men also involves the effort to understand how they were hurt in areas where they were hindered from experiencing feelings. This could also help them to realize the damage that was done to their ability to communicate their real needs, which hampered their ability to be intimate with others.

Shame remains the main culprit. It poisons self-love. Transformation requires allowing men to deal with the shame that so often accompanies straying from the restrictions of the past, and which sometimes tamps down inspiration.

Men need to claim the opportunity to get to know and learn how to express shame and free themselves to experience other emotions, such as loss and depression, and even joy, that have been buried over the lifespan. As this happens, they can begin to experience the nurturing that was missed, and this nurturing can reorient the individual man to a new part of himself.

Can any man develop the courage to face life's opportunities to change and reach out for help when stuck or overwhelmed? The people in this book have answered that question with a resounding, Yes! Some did it themselves using the unique happenstances of their own lives to ready themselves for change. Others found that a mentor can be a great support in helping them to internalize the changes they wanted, and facilitate concrete movement toward living out evolving new beliefs and behaviors.

The ability to see the value of investing the time and effort in forging a fresh path does not always come so easily. Still, everyone can succeed. A good therapist, coach, or mentor can help you achieve what you envision at your own pace.

Facing our fear of change (even for the better) and understanding that it's natural is a way of reaffirming our oneness with all things. Like a young bird leaving the nest for the first time, there's a hesitancy and a feeling of uncertainty. Can I do it? Will it be good for me? Reaching inside and connecting to his own desire to fly and seeing other birds who have succeeded gives him the confidence to act. Taking that chance is the difference between emotional starvation and spreading your wings.

The establishment of a safe zone or a place to let go with less fear will allow you the freedom you need to explore. You know you have hidden abilities and strengths, but you need the right encouragement to reclaim them. Most of the time there is not certainty with regard to what is safe and what isn't. Stay open and be courageous about taking reasonable risks. You never know for sure what you will learn, but you will.

I want to share an experience that influenced me when I was a young adolescent. Like most teenagers, I was trying to find my place in our group of friends. One day, my friend asked me to try something that he said might seem unusual. He asked me to sing a note and hold it, and he would harmonize with it. I asked him if he was kidding. I was afraid. Self-consciously, I blurted out a sound and he harmonized with it. We did it again. I was intrigued. Then, my brother joined us and we began doing three-part harmonies to old doo-wop songs. We'd sing in the streets, in the subways (there was a natural echo), and anywhere there were people to listen. At first, I felt shy. Boys don't sing like this! They play sports. Little did I know that this series of experiences would lead me on a musical journey that would be a kind of avocation for most of my life. I didn't know it then, but some very important life skills presented themselves to me in that moment.

What Tom Learned:

1. I learned that it was okay to move out of a very comfortable, safe space into something new and exciting. I took a chance. I let myself be exposed to something that most boys didn't do at the time.
2. Learning to harmonize involves concentration and being able to listen to other people as you progress through changes of movement in a song. Being attuned and maintaining confidence serve me well as a singer, a father, husband, and therapist!
3. The experience of achieving a goal as I worked in concert with other people was very satisfying and began to teach me cooperation. In the end, I learned something new and wonderful about myself that is still with me all of these decades later.

———————

We are exposed to so many events and situations that compel us to make choices. And every choice leads us in a new direction, sometimes by inches and sometimes by miles. What determines that choice is our "why," that thing we want or want to get away from. We determine what motivates us and then direct our passion to take us there. A bit of effort and then … once we start and we reach out for support, we find we are in new company, traveling alongside men and women who are also reaching out, fellow explorers, always learning and becoming.

ACKNOWLEDGEMENTS

No one writes a book on his own. You need lots of support and encouragement from people around you, people who believe in you and the work that you do. Thanks to my wife, Arlene for believing in me and my need to write and share my vision of representing men's opportunities for growth.

For my children who have challenged me, inspired me and expected the best of me. I thank you for your unconditional love and acceptance. And to my extended family, I value and appreciate all of the moments we have shared together. You have enriched my life experience and I will treasure that always.

To my editor, Suzi for all the work in keeping my message clear while staying true to the intended meaning of the various flavors and spirit of the men represented. Thanks as well to Suzi for her perceptive eye in representing the truth in the book's content.

And to Alex, my kindred spirit. Our journey together through music helped teach me the depth of life that is available for all men to experience.

To the many like Maggie, Fran, Carol, Estela, Sophia, Paul, Catherine, Ken, Kathy and both Donna's who have shared in many parts of my life's journey contributing to my growth as a man, I offer my sincerest thank you.

With gratitude to my Cornerstone group, Ray, Phil, Wayne, Jose, Mark and Marcel who for over 20 years have given me a place to work out my ideas about what kind of man I wanted to be.

I also am grateful for the knowledge and support of Philip J Guerin MD and David Chabot PHD, who served as my mentors and colleagues for many years, and are both master therapists. Their wisdom, sensitivity and excellent teaching expertise have taught many of us the art and critical skills of family therapy.

I want to express my appreciation to my colleague and friends, Adrienne and Karen for the 20 plus years that we worked and laughed together.

A special thank you to all my clients and friends who have contributed to this book. Their honesty, courage and openness in facing the various dilemmas in their individual roles as men, have made this book possible for us all to benefit.

Thanks to Stacy and Beverly who in their unique ways have encouraged me to write.

BIBLIOGRAPHY

Ashworth, D. Psychology blog, damonashworthpsychology.com – "How Have Intimate Relationships Changed Over the Years, and Where Does It Leave Us Now?" May 24, 2016.

American Psychological Association, www.apa.org "The Changing Role of the Modern-Day Father," Sept, 2009

Bowlby, J. & Spitz, R., "The Experience of Touch: Research Points to a Critical Role," *NY Times,* February 2, 1988.

Braswell, K. "Dealing with Anger from Having an Absent Father," *First Things First,* July 20, 2017.

Brown, B., "Daring Greatly." New York: Penguin Random House, 2015.

Farrell, W. "Why Fathers Matter," *First Things First.* April 2017.

Field, T. "Touch (a Bradford Book)". Massachusetts Institute of Technology 2001

Finkel, E. "*The All or Nothing Marriage*". New York, NY: Dutton, 2017.

Flores, A., R, Herman, Jody L, Gates, Gary J, & Brown, Taylor N. T. "How many Adults Identify as Transgender in the United States." *The Williams Institute: UCLA School of Law,* June 2016.

Francis, D. & Meaney, M. "The Touch of Life" in Positive Peace Project May 16, 2011.

Frankl, V. E. *Man's Search for Meaning.* Boston: Beacon Press, 1946/2006.

Fox, K. & O'Connor, J. "5 Ways Work Will Change in the Future," *The Guardian.* 2015. www.guardian.com

Gilligan, C. *In a Different Voice.* Cambridge: Harvard University Press, Reprint Edition, 1982.

Hawkins, M.D. & David R. *Power vs. Force: The Hidden Determinants of Human Behavior.* New York: Hay House Inc., 2002.

Henig, R.M. "Rethinking Gender," *National Geographic.* (Jan 2017): 48-103.

Howard, K. S., Burke Lefevre, J. E., Borkowski, J. G., & Whitman, T. L. "Father's Influence in the Lives of Children with Adolescent Mothers," *Journal of Family Psychology,* 20, (2006): 468-476.

Howard, K.S., Burke Lefevre, J.E., Borkowski, J.G., & Whitman, T.L. "The Positive Impact of Father Involvement," *National Fatherhood Initiative,* 2006.

Jeynes, W. "The Father Factor, First Things First: Do fathers really make a difference?" *National Fatherhood Initiative,* July 5, 2018.

Jones, J. "Why Physical Touch Matters for Your Well-Being," The Greater Good Science Center at UC Berkeley: *Greater Good Magazine,* Nov. 2018.

Krentzman, A. R. "What Is Spirituality?" U of Minnesota: *Taking Charge of Your Health and Well-Being,"* 2016.

Lin, Chunyi "Spring Forest Qigong-Level 1 *For Health" January 1, 2000.*

Millman, D. *The Way of the Peaceful Warrior: A Book That Changes Lives.* Tiburon, Calif.: HJ Kramer, New World Library, 2000.

Perel, E. The Gender Knot, 2018. www.thegenderknot.com - Season 3- "What's Next for Man and How Woman Can Help"

Perel, E. "On the Lives of Men," *The Psychotherapy Networker*, (Jan/Feb, 2019): 42-45.

Perel, E. Nov. 4th 2018 at Summit LA 18, YouTube, Feb. 2019. Famed Relationship Therapist Esther Perel Gives Advice on Intimacy, Careers, and Self-Improvement

Pruett, K. & Pruett M. Partnership Parenting: How Men and Woman Parent Differently- Why it Helps Your Kids and Can Strengthen Your Marriage September 1, 2009

Real, T. *I Don't Want to Talk About It.* New York: Scribner, 1997.

Rosin, H. The End of Men, *Atlantic Monthly*, Summer 2010.

Sax, L. *The Collapse of Parenting.* New York: Basic Books, 2016.

Sax, L. *Boys Adrift.* New York: Basic Books, 2017.

Simon, R. & Dockett, L. The Masculinity Paradox, *The Psychotherapy Networker,* (Jan/Feb 2019): 40-42.

Tiers, M. *The Anti-Anxiety Toolkit.* New York: Melissa Tiers, 2011.

Waldinger, R. "Harvard Longitudinal Study of Adult Development," Ted Talks, 2015.

Welwood, J. *Love and Awakening.* New York, Harper Collins, 1996.

Wilcox, W. B. The Distinct Positive Impact of a Good Dad, *The Atlantic*, July 14, 2013.

CPSIA information can be obtained
at www.ICGtesting.com
Printed in the USA
BVHW032137210621
610191BV00006B/102

9 781665 701006